Daniel J. Ferguson

MW00936972

Blessing's
Joni Ferguson

THE REMNANT

A Tribute to the Messy Middle Between
Church and Not-Church

DANIEL S. FERGUSON
&
LORI S. FERGUSON

WESTBOW
PRESS®
A DIVISION OF THOMAS NELSON
& ZONDERVAN

WestBow Press books may be ordered through booksellers or by contacting:

WestBow Press
A Division of Thomas Nelson & Zondervan
1663 Liberty Drive
Bloomington, IN 47403
www.westbowpress.com
844-714-3454

ISBN: 978-1-6642-6136-5 (sc)
ISBN: 978-1-6642-6137-2 (hc)
ISBN: 978-1-6642-6135-8 (e)

Library of Congress Control Number: 2022905089

Print information available on the last page.

WestBow Press rev. date: 03/24/2022

For Anna,
the beloved wife and daughter who never gives up on anyone

Contents

Preface ix

Chapter 1   It's Okay to Not Be Okay 1

Chapter 2   That's in the Bible? 23

Chapter 3   Orphans of God 34

Chapter 4   The Jesus Who Walks Away 44

Chapter 5   God the Promise-Breaker? 57

Chapter 6   Why You (Probably) Didn't Get a Personal
            Relationship with Jesus 67

Chapter 7   The Way of the Exile 78

Chapter 8   Fireside Chat 95

Chapter 9   Is the Church Really the Best God Can Do? 108

Chapter 10 The Revival 122

Chapter 11 The Party That Didn't Go So Well 143

Chapter 12 The Bride 155

Chapter 13 Forgiving the Church 167

Chapter 14 Hunting for Unicorns 177

Chapter 15 The Last Remnant 190

Afterword 201

Preface

The Line

There is a line between church and not-church. It exists ... somewhere. But how wide is the line? Big enough for a whole person to stand on? For a whole group? For a whole generation? And how blurry is it? Blurry enough for us to maybe not know where it begins and ends? Sure, there are some people who are definitely not in the church and some people who definitely are, but don't we all know people who are somewhere in the messy middle?

It's like the ocean. There's a part where you are certainly in it, and a part up the beach where you certainly aren't. But then there's this space in between where you can walk that's always shifting with each wave. That space is so holy that it doesn't even really have a name, but everyone can observe it and knows what it is. In terms of Christianity, it's an area where a person can exist in a messy middle somewhere between acceptance and rejection. It doesn't have a name, either.

In the Bible, whenever God brings down a wrath of some kind, he always leaves behind what he calls a "remnant." That word appears some sixty-seven times in the Bible, as early as Genesis, with threads all the way to Revelation, but mostly in the Old Testament prophets. It represents a piece of the population left over after a great calamity. This remnant often arrives into something they couldn't have imagined—a new nation with a new king and a new culture, a new way of living altogether. No one was left unchanged by it, regardless of their piety or previous position. This remnant was left behind in a place that always presented choices. Will they commit themselves wholly to the new reality, regardless of what it means about their previous identity? Or will they stalwartly stand on what they used to believe, even to the point of total rejection? Or is there a third option, something in the messy middle, somewhere along the shore between ocean and land, a place where they can both assimilate into the new culture and yet hold on to their prior principles?

It is little secret that the Christian church in the United States has suffered such a calamity. Just like the Israelites of old, it was a calamity of our own making. We pursued the idols of greed and power-lust, and God, just like he did with Israel, knocked us down to our knees, leaving behind a wake of people who find themselves in that messy middle, with one foot inside their old faith and the other in a wholly secular culture. We don't blame you for your position there. If anything, we greatly respect the mental and spiritual perseverance it takes to exist as you do. You have stretched your mind, heart, and soul to maintain your faith to some degree, even as you live in doubt and sorrow over the loss of the church family to which you belonged for so long. You probably feel worn thin, and you may be coming to your wit's end as to choosing how to live, or wondering if you even have to.

You're not alone. You see, we've been in this place too.

Daniel's Story

I almost put the letter in the mail. It was handwritten, some three pages long, explaining to my family why I was leaving my Christian faith for good. It was addressed; it was sealed; it was stamped. I even knew how I was going to do it, in phases. I planned on "coming out" (to borrow the phrase) to my brother-in-law first. He had left the faith for the most part too, so he would at least understand. He would probably know what to do next. Then I would write to my atheist brother and his wife. They would surely accept me as a religious refugee, or so I hoped. They weren't first because I feared they might laugh at me for the grief I felt over a faith they saw as ridiculous. But they were next. Then my sister, then my other sister, and then my parents, then finally my wife. I had a plan.

I had been a bad Christian. I was raised by wonderful religious parents. They didn't try to force faith onto me, nor did they compel me to make decisions I wasn't ready for. But I was so eager to please them that I consented to something I probably shouldn't have. I even planned a career in ministry, largely to make them happy. It definitely wasn't for me, though, as I lacked the moral integrity to lead God's people well. I committed every sin in the book on the path to my inevitable implosion. I gave in over and over again to the temptations of power, greed, deceit, and lust, an addict for attention. When I crashed (and I crashed hard), my parents were there for me. They took me in to let me lick my wounds. But I still feigned faith, to some degree, if only to make them happy and keep them off my back. I was so worried about my reputation with them that I continued to hide my doubts and mask my agony. I was left with nothing but fallen stars.

Along the way, I met a wonderful woman who loved Jesus with all her heart. She wrote letters to him every Saturday morning and believed to her core. I fell in love with her in mere minutes. It happened without my permission. If my decision had been rational, I probably wouldn't have chosen to. But love isn't rational. Our faiths didn't align; our values didn't align; our views of the world didn't align. But our hearts aligned all the same. She eventually fell in love with me too (it took some convincing), and we married before long. It was she who kept me going to church, who kept me reading the

Bible, and who kept me praying. Again, if only to make her happy, if only to keep up appearances and to keep her loving me.

That was the problem with my faith. It was almost always a head fake. I certainly understood the tenets of Christianity well (I went to seminary, after all), but the liar in me always created an image that I was more devout than I really was. With the same mouth that sang to Jesus, I slandered. With the same hands that were raised on Sunday mornings, I indulged myself on Sunday afternoons. I was a total hypocrite who burned every bridge along the way. If you had met me during this time, your every suspicion of Christians being charlatans would have been confirmed. I was a total imposter, even to my family and best friends.

But I knew deep down that something had to change. I couldn't ride the fence of faith for much longer. As they say, truth will out. So rather than let it out on its own, I decided for the first time that I was going to tell the truth about where I stood on God. I wrote the letter to my brother-in-law. I sealed it. I stamped it. I walked it to the mailbox. I opened the hatch. Then I hesitated. Something inside held me back. But it wasn't the size of it. It wasn't a desire to keep lying about my doubt. It wasn't the fallout that would invariably ensue from my family. No, I hesitated because for just a moment, for just a glimmer, I believed.

It wasn't much. It's not like I had a divine revelation. The clouds didn't part. I didn't hear a voice. No flashes of lightning. No peals of thunder. Rather, I felt an urge to simply throw the letter away in the trash can by my apartment complex's mailbox. Without even thinking, I followed that urge. Again, it happened without my permission. If I had been thinking rationally, I would have sent the letter and faced the consequences. But love isn't rational. And it was love that I was feeling. For the first time in my life, I clearly felt love for God. It wasn't fuzzy anymore. For just that brief moment, I rested in love.

You'll notice that I didn't say I felt love *from* God. That still hasn't happened to any recognizable degree. Rather, I felt love *for*

God. That moment didn't last very long, but it was enough to keep me going for a while. It was certainly enough for me to go to church the next Sunday. That's when everything changed.

My wife and I had spent years trying to find a church that fit. We had tried some and found corruption. We had tried others and been socially shunned. We had tried still others and found them too similarly lacking to the churches we grew up in. We even found one that spent more time talking about Buddha than Jesus. Weird. I had long since given up on ever finding one that would work, but my wife wanted to keep trying. If only to make her happy, I kept going with her. The very Sunday after I almost sent the letter, we again attended one that did not seem to fit. I mean, the music was too loud, the room was filled with haze, the worship leader looked like a cross between Ewan McGregor and Justin Timberlake, and the preaching was just basic Gospel with no particular exegetical depth or theological flourish.

But something happened there that I did not intend or expect. I fell in love. Yet again, it happened without my permission. I wasn't ready for it. And at once, there was this great conflict in my heart. One side knew that this church would probably burn me like all the others had for the last three years (and my whole life). But the other side was waiting for hope, just a small taste of it, that there might be healing and peace and joy left within the holy walls of God's community.

So we went back, and we went back again, and we met with someone on staff, and we started serving, and we started giving, and we started going to small groups. We just kept getting more and more involved. And bit by little bit, conversation by little conversation, healing started to occur. This church wasn't flawless by any means. It wasn't an anomaly that couldn't have been found anywhere else. And it wasn't the only place that we might have found a home.

But we did find a home, and the best spiritual decision of my life was choosing to commit to that home. Even when it hurt a little, even when I didn't want to go, even when I thought we might be getting burned again, even when I could peer beneath the rug and see the mess underneath it, we kept going. We kept committing. It was a challenge for my torn heart, and the choice to push all my chips in one last time was by no means easy. But I decided to bet it all, and I couldn't be happier that I did.

I still have doubts. I still have moments where I want to quit faith altogether. And I've still never felt God's presence, whatever that means. But now I at least have a community that's okay with all that. I never did tell most of my family about the letter (at least not until I wrote this), but that was one of the most pivotal moments of my life. It meant that I could finally learn to love God, not out of discipline but out of freedom. It meant that I could finally rest in something, even quasi-doubt mixed with quasi-faith, and have it be okay. It meant that I could finally have a Father in heaven, even if he still felt high up and far away.

Now, my story worked out in the end (for the most part). Maybe yours didn't or hasn't. That's okay. No one else's story is the same as mine, nor should it be. But no matter where you are, the challenge is this: keep trying. I know what it's like to feel like you have nothing left, that no part of your soul can stomach going back within a church's walls and hearing even one more song or one more sermon. I know what it's like to think, as the offering bucket goes by, that you're just throwing in good money after bad. I know what it's like for a communion tray to come down the row and wonder if anyone around you can tell that you're a fraud. I've been there. I know.

But I also know that God's not done with you, just like he's not done with me. A lot has changed in my life since that moment. I've struggled. I've strived. I've crashed and burned a couple of times too. But through it all, I keep going back to that moment at the mailbox, that crisis of decision. For good or ill, I chose Christ. I don't fault you if you haven't, or even if you wouldn't have in my shoes. But it's been enough for me to keep going, to keep reaching out for that invisible, untouchable God.

Maybe that's not your story, or at least not yet. Maybe it never will be. But I hope you'll keep reading, not because I'm trying to convince you of anything, but because I believe that I'm not the only one who's been through this. I've met too many other people in the messy middle to believe that I'm alone. It feels lonely sometimes, I'll admit, particularly at church, but there's a group out there, other people who stand on the line between acceptance and rejection, other people who pursue faith even amongst doubt. God told us to love him with everything we have, so if doubt is all you have, doubt is what you have to love him with. That's not bad, that's not heresy, and that's not hypocrisy. That's faith.

There is room within Christianity, even within many churches, for people like me, which means there's room for people like you too. Don't give up just because you haven't heard from God. Don't give up just because you haven't found that perfect church family. Don't give up just because you're standing at the mailbox, with trembling hands. Don't ever, ever give up.

Lori's Story

Hi, my name is Lori, and I'm part of the problem. Or I was, anyway. Maybe I still am. I felt called to the Christian vocation at age seventeen, and I really never looked back. I loved the church, warts and all, and as I continued to serve on church staffing, I learned the culture. At the time, churches were growing. They were adding full- and part-time ministry positions all over the place, and I was happy to be called by churches into them. I learned to talk the talk and walk the walk every step of the way. I loved organizing and programming events for the church, and I got really, really good at it. The trouble was that the focus was more on numbers, revenue, and bigger buildings, less on individual discipleship, and even less on God.

I'm a career minister, forty years and counting. I've been doing this gig for a long, long time. When I first started out as a civilian in the Air Force Chaplaincy, everything I touched seemed to turn to gold: every program, every initiative, and even little stuff like counseling relationships. It was so much fun. Then in 1992, my husband left the Air Force, and we moved near Nashville, Tennessee, to raise our four children. (The youngest is cowriting this book. His story is above.) This meant that I had to leave my civilian role in the chaplaincy and start working at regular churches.

Everything turned upside down. At one church where I was on staff, everything seemed fine at first, until it wasn't. I won't go into too many details, but suffice it to say that things got toxic pretty quickly.

So onto the next church, still in the greater Nashville area. This time, I was the Minister of Education. As it turns out, this church was resistant to a woman leading a ministry, for fear of … well, I don't know. One leader apparently spent all of his political capital just to hire me, a situation that led to my being dramatically underpaid and undervalued. Much of the inertia that was gained with the work I loved doing was lost in a very toxic tug-of-war of who could have more power. This was a basic staff-versus-laity leadership tug-of-war, and we spent most of our time dueling each other rather than reaching our community. Though my children had essentially grown up in this church, it was no longer a good idea for us to go there. It was simply too poisonous a work environment for me.

One more try. I started working specifically in children's ministry at that point, this time as an associate director at a larger (and much more affluent) Nashville church. My new boss had a wonderful reputation for her work at this church. The children's ministry program was large and flourishing. Or so I thought. This church didn't hire me full-time as promised, despite having ample funding for doing so. What was worse was that, in many cases, the requirements of the job far outpaced the twenty-nine hours per week that part-time work would have allowed for. I was stuck doing far too much work to get it all done, thereby regularly exceeding the hours (which they were happy to take for free), or else I had to leave the work undone, goals that I perceived I needed to meet or exceed to be seen as competent enough to keep my job. It was a lose-lose no matter how you sliced it. For years, I advocated and demonstrated the need for the church to simply hire me as a full-time employee, but I was always told they couldn't afford it. This from a church with millions in its annual budget.

As it turns out, my upward mobility was being limited due to some behind-the-scenes power struggles. It was personal. Office politics ... at a church. I learned after I left the church the sabotage that was taking place. I wish I never knew. It was hurtful not only to me and my family but also to our ability to do ministry for and with our community.

All of that happened just in the Nashville area. My husband's career eventually took us to Maryland, where I worked at several other churches over time, and then to Florida, where I worked at yet another. It was funny that each church had its precious gifts, abilities, and people who genuinely sought the Lord, but every one of them was also a huge mess. There is not a place that I have served that I do not have significant scars from hurt, disappointment, and many straight-up personal attacks and intentionally harmful actions.

Even with all the junk that happened, I learned some really wonderful (and hard) lessons. I met people along the way who were (and are) godly and have a vibrant and growing love for Jesus. I went to seminary, which gave me more perspective, training, humility, and courage. It was a subtle change, but God began to transform my heart. I could see his love for his church. To this day, even after everything that has happened to me, I refuse to give up on what God has not given up on. He has, for whatever reason, decided to redeem the world through his church, however messy and misguided that often tends to be.

All those years I spent developing programs and curriculum, and being congratulated for numbers, fell before me like a plastic trophy. Yes, I was successful by most metrics, but to what end? Every week forward, I would ask myself a different question: Is what we are talking about on Sunday making any difference to people's Monday? Or Tuesday? To real life? My heart was softened, and I found the things I had learned through some pretty painful experiences were fuel and knowledge that would uniquely wire me to know the truth about some of the dirtiest laundry in the church. I leaned in to be a part of the solution. I would be remiss if I did not say that I was not just a recipient of painful church experience; as I succeeded in leadership, I did my share of standing on the shoulders of other, more worthy people, and hurting others by my overconfident, self-propagating style. I shudder when I think back at some of the things I said and did in the name of the ministry. All I can say now is that I am sorry.

We can get good at giving ourselves excuses and passes for so many things in the name of ministry. Oh, but the bodies we leave along the way. Forgive us, Father.

The first four chapters of Paul's letter to the Romans explain how broken the world is, but then we get a beautiful turn in chapter 5: "But God" (v. 8). You probably know the rest of the verse. It's famous. It's quoted all the time, and since this book is geared toward people who grew up in churchland, you likely can cite it better than I can. Here it is, though, for good measure:

> But God demonstrates his own love for us in this: While we were still sinners, Christ died for us. (Romans 5:8)

That was true then, so I believe it's true now. If God was willing to bet the farm on our broken world before Jesus came to earth, why not today? Something tells me that, even with the Western church in decline (and it is just the American and European churches that are in decline at this point), God is not done in the West any more than he's done in the world at large. He has already redeemed a lost world, and he will do it again.

So why do I bet my life on the church, even when it has scarred me so much? Because Jesus did. He still bears those scars today, a testament to how much he loves his church and what he is willing to give up for it. If he won't give up, I won't, either. His love for the church needs to be our love for the church. He is fully aware of how broken we are.

Why We Only Talk about American Protestant Christianity

It's going to be incredibly obvious that in this book, we're only discussing Protestant Christianity in the United States. We do that for several reasons. First, we're American Protestants ourselves and always have been, and because we, sadly, have not spent sufficient time exploring other cultures' faith practices, we only feel qualified to talk about our own. By American Christianity, we typically mean Protestantism, again because this is the faith tradition to which we belong. We are not, and will not pretend to be, experts in any other kind of faith. We are deeply critical in this book toward white evangelicalism in particular (though we tend not to name it directly), not because we stand opposed to it on its own but precisely because we belong to it. We both come from a Southern Baptist tradition, though Lori became a United Methodist minister later in her career. Daniel grew up in the Southern Baptist church but has since dabbled mostly in evangelical nondenominational churches, which he notes aren't all that different from denominational ones.

We feel this is acceptable because a plurality of American Christians are Protestants, with the largest group being evangelicals. We specifically avoid discussing Catholicism in this work, even knowing that almost a quarter of American Christians are Catholic, because again, we are not experts in that faith tradition. Thus, when we talk about the "American church," we intend what it largely means in the American imagination: Protestant evangelicalism. We know that this is not the whole story; the global community of believers, and even those within the United States, is ethnically and ideologically diverse. By discussing American Christianity, we don't mean to exclude other forms from consideration; we're just not experts in them.

Why We Use the Bible in This Book

It won't take you too many chapters to realize that we rely heavily on the Protestant Christian Bible to make some of our points. We do this realizing that the Bible may be a sore subject for many of the people we're trying to influence most. However, as we'll discuss later, just because you no longer believe in something doesn't mean it no longer has any gravitational pull on you. We suspect that many of our readers still have some measure of belief in biblical principles like justice, compassion, forgiveness, love, and faithfulness. You may have first learned about these values in the Bible, and they didn't suddenly disappear from your heart just because you walked away from the church.

We use the scriptures primarily because we believe the whole of the biblical narrative points to Jesus, whom we still, after all our journeys, believe to be the saving force in this world. That may not be where you're at, and we get that. But we suspect that you haven't fully released its holy words from your heart and that they still have some resonance for you, if not practical application. After all, if someone's life is so impactful that most of the world literally marks time differently based on his arrival into the world, it might be wise to listen to what he has to say, even if you don't believe he's God or that there's even a God to be found out there at all.

Third, we employ scripture because it, unlike almost anything else we've ever read, explores the full weight of the human experience. It ranges from our highest ecstasies to our darkest depressions, and everywhere in between. It delves deep into the human psyche and illuminates what's at the core of all our souls. In this regard, it's rather like the collected works of Shakespeare, but since the Bible is more appropriate for our topic, we focus on it.

We also use the Bible because it's sort of a home base for us and, we suspect, for many of you. Even though we struggle with many of its difficult implications, we still find it to be a treasure trove of wisdom, guidance, and memory. We do our best to present its stories and passages in a fresh light, focusing particularly on the narratives themselves. You'll find that we add some of our own embellishments to the scriptures and make some interpretive leaps based on the premise of this book, which you may not have heard before. That's all intentional on our part, as we seek to bring these passages to you in new ways and toward our ultimate goal: a fuller, richer understanding of what it's like to be part of the remnant we discuss in this book.

What is that remnant? Well, keep reading.

1

It's Okay to Not Be Okay

The Calamity

Meteors didn't fall from the sky. A great flood didn't come. Lightning struck nothing. There was no horn blown from heaven, nor from hell. The dead stayed dead. The living stayed living. None of the predicted events came true. Yet the end was nigh. A great calamity had befallen God's people, a terrific horror. They were no longer the majority.

Or so it seemed. Maybe not. In 2014, a Gallup poll indicated that less than half of Americans (41 percent) attend church weekly. Yet a Pew poll taken the next year indicated that 75 percent of Americans consider themselves Christians. That means there's a massive middle ground of people who believe that they follow Jesus but don't go to a church activity regularly. A 2007 *Christianity Today* poll breaks down Christianity in the United States this way:

- Nineteen percent of Christians are active Christians, meaning they believe salvation comes through Jesus, attend church regularly, read their Bible, and evangelize often.
- Twenty percent are professing Christians, meaning they believe salvation comes through Jesus, attend church regularly, and participate in personal spiritual development, though they do not invest heavily in church services or direct evangelism.
- Sixteen percent are liturgical Christians, who recognize the authority of the church and attend regularly.
- Twenty-four percent are private Christians, only about one-third of whom attend church ever. They profess to believe in God and perform good deeds, but they do so outside of a church context.
- Twenty-one percent are cultural Christians who do not consider Jesus to be essential to salvation, instead seeing many paths to God, but they still call themselves Christians when asked.

This study suggests that there's a huge middle ground, a great big blurry line between church and not-church that makes up roughly 45 percent of people who claim the Christian religion as their own. That's over seventy million American adults. Many people claim that those people aren't Christians at all and shouldn't be counted, leaving, at most, half of the remaining people. And frankly, that study is outdated. A more recent survey (Pew 2019) indicates that Protestantism in particular has taken a massive hit in the last decade, dropping from just over half of the American population (51 percent) in 2007 to just 43 percent in 2019, all while the population of the so-called "nones" (people who claim no religious affiliation) has increased by almost half its size.

A great calamity has befallen (and continues to befall) the American church. So many pastors have pontificated on what has happened that you'd be right to ask what good another book on this topic would do. While some of those works are interesting and provide great insight, what hasn't been discussed thoroughly is the church's part in all this. Many authors seem to think that culture won them over or that their faith was never real in the first place or, at most, that the church simply wasn't engaging or relevant enough. But we argue that the reason many people left is the harm the church did. They didn't leave the church behind. We left them behind.

There is a growing population of postchurch people who left because of us. According to the earlier study, 8 percent of Generation Xers who used to claim Christianity now don't in just the last decade, all while 6 percent more claimed themselves as unaffiliated. With the millennials, the change is even starker: 16 percent have dropped the title "Christian" in the last decade, while 13 percent have taken up the label "unaffiliated." We believe it wasn't MTV that won them over, nor the liberal media, nor sex, nor drugs, nor rock and roll. They weren't pulled from the faith. They were pushed. By us.

This massive change didn't happen overnight, nor did it happen by accident. You can think they left, just to leave. You can think they were just snowflakes who couldn't handle the honest truth. And you can even think they were never really believers in the first place. But you'd be wrong. From our experience and interviews, many (if not most) of these people were at one time God-honoring, Bible-believing, truth-speaking, neighbor-loving, friend-evangelizing Christians. Not all but many. They didn't usually learn their culturalized faith from their parents. They took it on as a mechanism to protect themselves from us. This is especially true of conservative evangelical churches, and it's part of why the Moral Majority of the United States has mostly imploded. Sure, it technically dissolved in the late 1980s, but just look at the quote from founder Jerry Falwell when it did: "Our goal has been achieved. The religious right is solidly in place."

Boy, was he ever right (pun intended). But before you think that's a good thing, just look around you at the Christian landscape of today. What happened? Have the churches grown and become more inclusive, creating a safe place for people to chase after God? Largely not. Many of the churches we grew up in—indeed, many of the churches that are still clinging on for dear life—are what we call wedge churches. These are the ones that intentionally drive a wedge between themselves and the culture around them. For a long while, there was a comfortable middle space between church and not-church, and that space existed within our walls, where people could pursue Jesus on their own terms, with the help of those who were there.

But then a new movement showed up in the late 1970s. The Moral Majority's explicit goal (meaning they actually said this out loud to people) was to mobilize Christians into a political force that would elect conservatives to high office. This created a definitive sense that certain people belonged in Christian circles and others didn't. If you didn't believe that abortion was always murder, you were out. If you didn't believe homosexuality was always sinful, you were out. If you didn't believe women should stay in the home and remain quiet, you were out. If you were different, if you didn't go through the meat grinder, if you didn't act, vote, and give like the rest of them, you were out.

It's not like those positions weren't well intentioned. The church has not necessarily been wrong on all these issues. Our problem as authors is not with the church having an opinion, even a bad one. Our problem comes when churches abuse their opinions on various issues to deny love and care to individuals. Jesus's commands have little to do with our squabbles and more to do with our compassion. When the church continued to fail to be kind, many recognized that for what it was: love of power over people.

So, unsurprisingly, many of those people saw themselves out, most notably those who were children or teenagers at the time. At the same moment they were trying to find their identities and adapt to their changing culture, they were forced through prominent pressure to conform to a certain set of beliefs and attitudes. They loved Jesus with all their hearts—for a while. Then they associated

Jesus with the church they grew up in, and they started to rebel, creating a whole messy middle that exists today as an albatross. They are the remnant of our greatest mistake. We think they simply need a revival. But they don't need it. We do. We abandoned them. We abandoned the mission of Jesus and the kingdom of heaven for the fleeting approval of fleeting men. Power became our idol.

And just like God did with ancient Israel, we are paying the price for our idolatry with this great calamity. No one has removed us from our churches (nor is that likely to happen), but they have evicted us from the temples of their souls. Our church doors aren't being closed by force but by necessity. And we are losing our grip on the very thing we chased in the first place: social influence. Sure, the religious right is still having its day politically as a result of its successes a generation ago, but is that really what we want? Political sway? Mere earthly power? Is what we want just to win the next election, to appoint the next judge, and to swear in the next president? That seems small and petty. As Jesus puts it, "What good is it for someone to gain the whole world, yet forfeit their soul?" (Mark 8:36). What we have done is nothing short of arrogant idolatry.

The earthly power that the Moral Majority promised was just that: earthly. And yeah, it worked for a while, and it continues to work somewhat to this day. But we Christians would be fools if we were satisfied with today's situation. Having political power means nothing if we lose masses of souls along the way. You can legislate all you want, but you can't vote people into the kingdom of heaven. There has been a rebellion against us, not because we are being persecuted but because we have become the persecutors. We did it when we gay-bashed. We did it when we told women they were murderers for getting an abortion. We did it when we made fun of transgender people. We did it when we thumped people's heads with Bibles and shouted God's wrath from the streets. And we did it when we framed people's choices in terms of heaven and hell. We became the persecutors.

5

That's because, as we stated in one of our other books, *So Loved the World*, we were never supposed to be a moral majority but rather a missional minority. What good is it for 75 percent of Americans to claim themselves as Christian if half of those want nothing to do with the church? Where is the power in that? Where is the mission?

So, yes, no meteors fell from the sky to crash into our church buildings, but as Jesus says to the church in Ephesus, "Consider how far you have fallen! Repent and do the things you did at first. If you do not repent, I will come to you and remove your lampstand from its place" (Revelation 2:5). The church must repent. We must repent of our idolatry and arrogance. We must repent of our pursuit of power instead of purpose. And we must repent for losing so many of God's children by thrusting them out into the cold. We must repent or else totally lose our ability to testify the resurrection of Christ to the world. We must repent or else lose our lampstand for good.[1]

Fragments of a Shattered Masterpiece

But wait. It gets worse.

Not only did we push people away from the church, but we also pushed churches away from each other. Protestants in particular are guilty of what many call denominationalism but what we call fragmentation. We use that word because what used to be a beautiful stained-glass window is now a pile of broken shards scattered on the floor, each trying to occupy its own space. There are over sixty denominations just within evangelicalism, with mainline Protestantism, Catholicism, Pentecostalism, Orthodox, and many others besides. We can't seem to agree on much. Sure, with a religion of 2 billion people worldwide, there are going to be some cultural differences, but do we really need sixty denominations of American

---

[1] A note for those who don't delve into Revelation that often (which we completely understand): This passage deals with a church's ability to witness to the good news about Jesus. If it's not doing that, then it's really not a church, which is why Jesus says he will take away their lampstand, or their ability to be a witness.

evangelicalism alone? We have argued in the past that there needs to be a great diversity of thought within the church, but we claimed that this diversity must be within an individual church, not only within the scope of Christendom itself.

Modern American fragmentation is akin to the political practice of gerrymandering, where representative districts get divided up in such a way as to create "safe" seats for a particular party. Both Republicans and Democrats are guilty of this. Just look at the bizarrely shaped federal districts in North Carolina or Maryland, and you'll see our point. Gerrymandering is not only bad for districts remaining diverse and competitive but also because its cumulative effect is to create more polarized groups. A moderate Republican can't get elected in a gerrymandered district because the primary competition in that district is too far to the right, and the same thing happens on the Democratic side too, with the left. The result is that there are fewer and fewer moderates in each successive election, leaving just two poles of people shouting at each other across a messy middle that hates them both. Between that, cable news, toxic leadership, and social media, we have become more polarized and divided than at any time since the Civil War. A pox on both our houses.

The same thing has happened in churches. We continue to fracture and divide, creating spaces that are safe for people who believe the same thing as everyone else in that particular church. If you don't like one church's view of baptism, then go to the Southern Baptists. If you don't like another's view of predestination, then go to the Lutherans, and so on. We have created massive organizations of Christians who on the surface show theological and practical differences, but in reality are just spaces for people who already agree with each other to commiserate about why everyone else is wrong.

While he was in high school, Daniel used to date a young woman who was of the Church of Christ. Daniel was raised Southern Baptist, but he went with this young woman to her church a few times to bolster their relationship. Invariably, every time he went, the sermon or Sunday school lesson bashed Baptists. It was like they were waiting for him. Most of the time, the problem stemmed from using musical instruments as part of the worship service (that's a big no-no for the Church of Christ), and Daniel was always stared at like he was some sort of leper. Now, imagine that for a first-time guest. Oh, that's right. *There weren't any.* That was by design. The only new people who ever came to that church were people who had just moved into the area who already belonged to that denomination. But as far as new, organic growth goes, that church was effectively dead.

Again, that wasn't by accident. That church, and many like it (including ours at the time), only included people who were already like them. In a tiny town of about four thousand people, there were probably about twenty churches, meaning that if every soul in the city went to church (certainly not the case), there would be only two hundred at each one. Some were larger (three hundred or so), most were smaller (fifty or so), but hardly any was missional, even our own. What they were was denominational, fragmented, a stained-glass masterpiece shattered from the inside. We had a city full of churchgoers who had no mission whatsoever. There were many Christians, but there was no real sense of purpose. We were Christians for the sake of being Christians, baptizing only our children (if that) and reaching out only to those who already agreed with us. Such is the disgrace of denominationalism. We lost two whole generations (and now their children) to our folly.

Now, we're not saying that everybody has to agree. Hardly. What we are saying is that there needs to be plenty of room within one church's community for loyal dissent. We must be able to coexist, not only from a distance, but within the same walls. In Christ, there is no Lutheran, no Methodist, no Catholic, and no Baptist. There are only the love of Jesus and the mission of the kingdom of heaven. If we're out on a venture to expand our denomination's influence, then we are completely missing the endeavor of Christ.

Before you think this is about other churches, really take a look at your own. Even if it's nondenominational (a growing trend), does it really accept outsiders? Not just people who look different, but people who act differently? Believe differently? For a time, both of us lived in Maryland after having lived in Nashville. We figured that because Maryland was a bluer state in general that we would find more Democrats and other liberals in evangelical churches, just because of the demographics involved. However, the opposite seemed to be true. Most of the churches we attended (separately and together) seemed to be ideological pigeonholes where people all voted the same way and believed the same thing. The minority of conservatives in the state had safeguarded themselves in tiny Christian communities throughout the region, walling themselves off from the more liberal, secular world around them.

Nondenominational churches, especially church plants, have become such a large trend that they are almost a denomination unto themselves. They may not be ideologically or financially related, but they have a surprising number of practical and theological similarities. Because they're all independent of each other, their theology is just as divisive as any standardized denomination. There's nothing wrong with any of these churches as such, but we argue that they represent a real fragmentation in the form of a shadow denomination, a Generation X-ish response to the divisiveness of the church they grew up in, only to realize that what they are doing is also a division. Instead of helping churches become better, they're often just creating new churches to replace the old ones. That's not usually unifying. It's often just another division. There can be good in those churches. Those are usually the best churches around in terms of programming. But do they represent a vibrant change in the landscape of American Christianity? Usually not.

This is precisely why so many people feel burned and left behind by the American church. We are so petty so often that we look patently ridiculous. We once heard some students and their adult leaders at a Protestant Christian youth camp making fun of Mormons for what they believe. We're not here to comment on whether or not Mormons are Christians. That's not our point.

Rather, what we heard was these kids and adults remarking that what Mormons believe was ludicrous and that nobody could truly believe in something so outlandish.

Except you know who believes something even weirder? Christians. As Urban Dictionary puts it, Christianity is "the belief that a cosmic Jewish Zombie who was his own father can make you live forever if you symbolically eat his flesh and telepathically tell him you accept him as your master, so he can remove an evil force from your soul that is present in humanity because a rib-woman was convinced by a talking snake to eat from a magical tree." You may think that definition is somewhat bigoted (it is), but what part of it is untrue? Jesus is both God and man (cosmic), a Jew who was raised from the dead (zombie), who claimed to be one with his own Father (John 10:30), who offers eternal life (John 3:16), and so on. There's nothing in that definition that's not true of us. It's just framed in the weirdest possible light. But what we believe is, in fact, odd. Other denominations and religions aren't inferior just because they're strange to us. And just because we believe our faith to be true doesn't make it any less absurd (see 1 Corinthians 1:18).

We have left behind whole generations of former Christians because we refused to have what Simon Sinek calls "existential flexibility" (*The Infinite Game*). We were so rigid in our various models that we didn't stay true to our singular mission: "to seek and to save the lost" (Luke 19:10). We thought that theological purity mattered. It mostly doesn't. We thought that the right practices and methods mattered. They mostly don't. We thought that good programming mattered. It mostly doesn't. What does matter is love, and when it comes to loving people who are different from us, we have failed spectacularly for generations. We were bitter and mean instead of caring and compassionate. In the fight for ninety-nine more sheep, we forgot the one.

Exiles and Leftovers

Who is that one sheep? Well, in this case, there are many. There's a massive and messy middle in between church and not-church, as we discussed earlier. Who are these people? What are they like? What do they believe? And what could win them back?

The first issue most researchers take on is trying to define Christianity. In doing so, they often draw hard lines between who is in and who is out, with little room for margin. The Christian research agency Barna, for example, holds a rather exclusive view of who is Christian and who isn't, with a defining bent toward evangelicalism as the highest form of faith. They believe that to be a "true" Christian, you must hold to the following seven tenets:

1. You believe in absolute moral truth.
2. You have an orthodox view of God.
3. You say that religious faith is personally important to you today.
4. You feel a responsibility to share your religious beliefs with others.
5. You believe the Bible is accurate in all of the principles it teaches.
6. You believe that Jesus didn't sin in his time on earth.
7. You believe that Satan is not a symbol but a living being.

What strikes us most about this list is that there's no core Christian theology here. There's no mention of the death and resurrection of Christ and not even a wink at the indwelling of the Holy Spirit or the forgiveness of sins, all central Christian tenets. There's not even an homage to heaven and hell. What seems to be important here is a personal, mental assent to a set of beliefs that are, at best, within the realm of question in Christianity. But we have postured ourselves so adamantly on these tenets (and a few others) that on the blurry line between church and not-church, we have erected a stone fence that people must climb over to be part of us.

11

Many have stared at that fence for a long time and simply given up. It wasn't culture that built that wall. It was us. That wall has separated families, pitted brother against brother, set about a massive amount of divisiveness, and caused social and cultural wars. This isn't new or even exclusive to evangelicalism, but like it or not, when many postchurch Americans think of Christianity, that's what they're thinking of. It's something that rejected more than it accepted, that defined itself by what it was against instead of what it was for, and that pushed instead of pulled. After it churned up the masses in its fiery engine, it left behind a huge wake of souls. That may not be a fair characterization of Christianity as you know it, but ask almost anyone who has left. That's largely what they see and feel.

The next issue that faces us when we try to define the postchurch group comes in why they left individually. There's a whole host of reasons why people say they left, but why they began leaving is a whole other story. In all the interviews we have done of postchurch people (literally all of them), the process of their leaving began with a personal and emotional injury to them or a loved one. They didn't (at least, not at first) give up on belief or faith in God. They gave up instead on belief or faith in the church as an institution. They associated their pain with the people within our holy walls.

So large is the problem that one Barna study found 37 percent of non-churchgoing Americans avoid church because of negative past experiences in church communities or with church people. That's almost two out of every five. This isn't some theoretical or minor group. This is a massive population. According to their research, it's over 24 million American adults. We have met a fair number of these people personally, and all of their journeys away from the faith, or even away from God entirely, began with such a moment. A moment where people—Christians who claimed to follow Jesus—offered hate instead of love, rejection instead of acceptance, or criticism instead of compassion. These are the people who went to church as kids, attended the youth camps, wore the t-shirts, sang the songs, believed the core tenets, and loved Jesus with everything they had, until the church told them they were doing it wrong, they weren't good enough, and God didn't love them back. After all, if the church didn't, how could he?

Just like they were supposed to do, they associated the church with Jesus (see 1 Corinthians 12:27), and so when we squashed their souls, they interpreted that as Jesus doing it. Think about that. It's no wonder they no longer want his name having anything to do with theirs. They like Christ; they just don't like Christians. So they've started to dissociate themselves from us, and piece by little piece, they will separate their souls from their Savior.

The Six Stages of Grief

For many of us, leaving the church, or even considering it, feels like a death. We grew up with the institution being so much a part of our lives that removing it is like cutting out a vital pound of flesh. To some people, it's like a tumor; to others, it's like an organ. Either way, it's a profound experience that can cause great grief, and like with the grief of a lost loved one, often we have to process this sorrow in stages.

One of those stages (often the first) is denial. Denial means refusing to believe that something has changed. Many people get stuck here because their biggest response to the church at first is that it was all silly and unnecessary to begin with, so what's the big deal with choosing against it? This is short-sighted and naïve for most. For those who didn't grow up in church, it's no big deal for them to stay at home. They didn't lose anything but an opportunity. But for those who had church as a major part of their lives, cutting it out has profound implications. Maybe it means you no longer believe in a God with whom you once claimed to have a deep relationship. Maybe it means giving up on a meaningful set of emotional worship experiences you now consider frivolous. And maybe it means letting go of the substantial ties you spent a decade building up with people who loved you and whom you loved in return. No matter what, a whole piece of your identity, something you used to define yourself and your place in the world, has come shattering down. Denial is not a long-term option.

The reason most people pass through denial as one of the stages of grief is simply out of shock. There's suddenly a huge hole in your heart where something used to be. Something big. Something important. And now it's gone. In the case of leaving the church, this vacuum was a choice, but so are many painful breakups. Just because they represent a free choice doesn't mean they aren't agonizing. At first, there may be a sense of relief, as if a great weight has been lifted, and it's because of this that leaving the church can feel euphoric. But that pleasure is often fleeting, and it leaves in its wake a sense of emptiness that people seek to fill. For many, this filling takes the form of once prohibited behaviors and activities previously regarded as sinful, but this is grasping after the wind. It's not meaningful, and it usually doesn't represent who we want to become in the long run. It's merely a rebellion and an addictive behavior that we so often confuse with freedom.

The most obvious (and probably the most common) confusion comes from sex. The American church has largely done such a poor job communicating what it believes about sex that when many people leave the church, their first actions are to pursue suppressed sexual desires. It feels liberating for a while, but it almost always seems wrong in the long run. That's because sex isn't a substitute for real connection, and once that time of pleasure has expired, it so often leaves one feeling guiltier, emptier, and drier in the soul. That's not the puritanical church speaking; that's our conscience. That's denying the problem instead of facing it head-on. Denial is useful for a time in terms of shock absorption, but it is a stage that must be grown beyond. Remaining there too long is only a tool for self-delusion and not growth.

Once people have gone through denial, the next most common phase is anger. This is also the most common phase for people to revert to during their grieving process of losing the church in their lives. So many people have been hurt for so long that it seems morally just to feel a certain outrage against the machine that engineered that pain. We're not wrong to feel that. Anger can be a perfectly valid, even necessary emotion. Anger can be the fuel for the fires that burn down tyranny and oppression. Anger can be the engine of a righteous rebellion. Without anger, we would never think to oppose wrongdoing. Anger can even be a Christian feeling, as we understand God's wrath against sin carried out on the perfect Christ to be a necessary tenet of the faith. Anger can be good.

For a while. Anger all too quickly sours into bitterness and hostility. Anger must be kept in a cool, dry place for it to be used at the appropriate time, but leave it out in the heat, and it spoils so rapidly that you won't even recognize it before long. Anger has a way of bringing out the extremes in us. It can lead us to holy indignation against an evil power, but it can also lead us to become that evil power ourselves. Whenever we become angry, we must watch ourselves so we do not become like the very thing that makes us furious. We have all seen far too many times the story of a person who righteously rebels against tyranny only to become a tyrant in much the same regard. The most common place for this is in politics, where each side takes a position that opposes the other, often angrily, but besides the policy differences, they are remarkably similar in their approaches. The stiff legalism of the right is usually matched by the arrogant snobbery of the left, each group enforcing norms and beliefs among their respective constituents even as they oppose the others' enforcement of its own. In opposing each other in outrage, they have become like each other in form.

The same thing often happens when it comes to personal anger against the church. We may think the church was too puritanical, but we think less of people who choose to wait until marriage to have sex. We may think the church was unnecessarily dogmatic, but we reject from our presence and attention those who don't share our own beliefs. We may think of the church as restrictive and uncompassionate, but we often fail to have compassion for those who are still within it. In remaining angry, we become blind to our likeness to the very thing against which we rebelled. Little is more dangerous for a nation than replacing one tyrant with another, and similarly, little is more dangerous for a person than replacing one oppressive set of beliefs with another. Saying, "You must be like us to be with us," is exactly the sort of thing that made us angry at the church in the first place.

Like with denial, anger is a stage, not a landing point. It's easy to revert to, and it's healthy to go through it (even multiple times), but if we're going to grow past our pain and become the wholehearted people we all want to be, then anger must not be where we end our journey. Go through it, work with it, and grow from it, but do not rot in it. For that is exactly what it will do to you if you let it.

After anger, most people go through a stage called bargaining. Bargaining is where you try to deal with the pain of your loss through replacements and substitutes. In people dealing with their mortality, this often includes reaching out to God, or some other divine figure, and making a bargain for their lives, hence the name. "Lord, I'll give up drinking if you just spare my life." That sort of thing. Bargaining is a reaction to pain in that we'd rather feel almost anything else, so we try to satisfy ourselves with other things. While bargaining can take on a literal form in terms of prayers or offerings, it more often manifests as substitution, where we try to replace the thing we lost with another thing. In terms of the loss of a regular church gathering, we often try to substitute in a new group, one that we think will love us for who we are. There is nothing wrong with this. If the church has hurt you, trying to find group companionship is a healthy action.

The problem arrives, however, when we insulate ourselves with only like-minded people, particularly when those people all share the same outrage that we do. That can be helpful for a time, but a group defining itself by what it's against instead of what it's for is inherently dangerous. It's the same thing you were mad at the church for. This is most prevalent on social media, where there are many groups for people to vent their anger and tell their stories about how the church has hurt them, for their pain to be co-experienced. While there is some benefit to this in the short term, it often descends into bitterness and sarcasm, which have no place in a whole heart. We may feel vindicated by the fact that our experience is shared by so many, but there are few long-term benefits to this kind of revenge. We complain, we moan, we groan, but in that, we do not grow. Throwing communal pity parties feels sweet for a time, but it soon sours into pettiness, hypocrisy, and being angry for the sake of being angry—all things you probably left the church because of.

With that in mind, bargaining is a good stage to arrive at because it means you're searching for something, something you've lost and need to find again. Just make sure you don't let that something define you on its own terms.

After bargaining, many people sink into depression. This isn't necessarily the clinical depression that requires psychiatric treatment, but rather a stage of grief where a person is despondent and emotionally distressed. This is when we start to deal with grief because we can't avoid it anymore. The hole in our life has become a festering pit, and it needs cleansing before it will heal. Don't be fooled; just because you might believe that the church was preaching a false narrative doesn't mean that narrative lacks a hold on you. It was important to you. It had, and likely still has, a gravitational pull on you. Saying it never mattered is denial. Saying it's wrong to have mattered is anger. Saying it never should have mattered is bargaining. But depression forces us to come to terms with the fact that it did matter. In some way, the God you thought was so real seems to have died. You must grieve that death as you would a close friend.

Depression is a good phase to be in because it means you're beginning to work through the emotional and spiritual cut you've experienced. Denial ignores it. Anger rejects it. Bargaining avoids it. But depression enhances it. It will hurt—a lot. It will be agonizing. There's no avoiding it, and that's precisely the point. You can no longer avoid seeing that you've changed, that your world has changed, that your soul has changed. You may be questioning what being you even means now without religion to help you forge an identity. Religion was the very thing that made you who you were for so long that losing it is like losing yourself. Sit in that. Breathe in that. Grieve that. You've lost a friend, even if that friend was only just yourself. Something dramatic has shifted. As Charles Templeton, the great evangelist turned agnostic, once admitted, you probably miss Jesus.

It's okay to feel this pain. It doesn't make you less of a Christian, less of an agnostic, or less of a human. It doesn't make you less of anything. It makes you more. This stage of depression finally allows what matters to shout to you in your pain. Whether that's God or not is not our business as authors. We think it probably is, in many cases. But what matters is that you find some form of truth, even if that's just a truer sense of who you were, are, and are becoming. Depression can help with that.

But like anger, depression can also be quite sticky and bittersweet. So many people have defined themselves by their pain rather than their principles. This is, in the long term, bad for the soul. If we're thinking of this as a death, it's a problem that many people grieving a loss believe that if they leave the depression stage, they've lost their connection with their loved one for good. They feel guilty for moving on, and so they get themselves stuck in the rut of depression for a long time, as if that's going to keep the memory of the dead alive. In the same way, you may feel a sense of guilt for letting yourself move on from this stage. Because it's so defining and noteworthy, many people think they have to remain here, or else they'll lose their identity.

Make no mistake. That is letting your pain define you, which we doubt is what you want. You'd probably rather let your character define you, your quiet inner strengths. Pain does nothing but shout, which is why it's so deafening and seemingly identifying, but it's our soft voice that's the real us. We don't truly want to live in depression any more than we want to live in denial, anger, or bargaining. We want to be set free, to lose the bonds that have entangled us, and to move on.

That's why the next stage, acceptance, is so important. It's not easy to get here, nor is it any easier to stay. Acceptance is not forgetting the loss, or even necessarily moving on from the feelings of grief. Acceptance is, rather, understanding that reality has changed and will continue to stay changed, likely forever. Your new reality will forever impact your life and relationships. Even if you do eventually decide to return to church, you will never be the same dewy-eyed, youthful congregant you once were. You won't even really be the same person. You may never walk through a church's doors again, and that might be okay, but you are a new human for having gone through the trauma and loss. You may look back at your church experience as good, necessarily formative, and uplifting, but even if you return, that same feeling may never come back to you. And if you stay at home on Sunday mornings instead, you might still reflect fondly on some of your past. That's not a reversion any more than remembering the loss of a loved one is.

You may even still practice some of your faith independently, with actions like praying and reading the Bible. That doesn't mean you've slipped back into anything, and it doesn't make you any less of a religiously "unaffiliated" person, for whatever that's worth. Rather, it makes you what you are, someone who is in between church and not-church, and there's nothing inherently wrong with that. You moved on from your religious background probably because it was a source of some kind of trauma for you or for someone you love. Leaving that shouldn't make you feel guilty. Rather, acceptance means that you've come into your feelings wholeheartedly. You're not ignoring the pain, you're not revolting against it, you're not trying to negotiate with it, and you're not stuck in it. You're dealing with it head-on. And that's good.

The real trick with acceptance, however, is in taking responsibility for your actions. In the same way that we should not impose the abuse you suffered on your children, saying, "That's how I was raised, so it's okay," we must not carry forward what happened to us at church on the world around us. Where the church may have been judgmental, we must be gracious. Where it may have been puritanical, we must be liberating. Where it may have been abusive, we must be just. Where it may have been hypocritical, we must be righteous. Giving up on corporate faith does not relieve us of the individual duties of being good and healthy people. That's where acceptance comes in. It means taking responsibility for your feelings and the consequences of your actions. The church may never be a part of your life again, but its memory can be a positive companion in your days to come, at the very least having taught you resilience and perseverance through the pain.

The final stage of grief, and the one least often reached, is called finding meaning. This stage may not be familiar to you because it's only just recently been researched in the last decade or so, but it provides an important sense of finality to the grieving process that is relevant to our discussion of leaving the church. Many people don't reach this phase when it comes to church simply because their environment won't let them. Our popular culture has so thoroughly minimized Christianity to a laughingstock and a leech on our society (some of which is the fault of Christians) that most people who have left the church don't feel socially or emotionally capable of finding meaning in their pain. They're just not given the room to do it. It may not even occur to them to try. But that is a collective state of mixed denial, anger, and bargaining, a desperate hope to bury what once mattered so much into a casket that will never again see the light of day.

The more evolved approach, however, is to discover some sense of purpose for the grief. This isn't allowing the pain to define you, but this is allowing you to define your pain. It's not enough to dismiss your church experience as silly hype. That's reductive denial talking. Likewise, it's not enough to become bitter, to bargain, or to brood. Like it or not, there was some reason you went through your pain, and in the same way, there is some reason you've gone through grief. Giving up on church is a loss, often a tragic one, but it doesn't have to leave you in pieces. Gathering up those shards and reimagining them into a beautiful mosaic is still an option.

This is where we draw deep respect for those who have deconstructed and then reconstructed their faith. This is ultimately what Daniel had to do. He had to give up on believing for a long while and then tried to put all the pieces back together again. What he practices now looks something like traditional Christianity in form, but what used to be trite and ritualistic has taken on all new meanings for him as he has rediscovered a path toward God and the church. Through it all, he has found that his agony wasn't meaningless; he went through his pain so he could help others go through theirs, regardless of where they fall on the spectrum of faith.

Lori has a similar story, though she did not go through a period of faith deconstruction. All the same, she was hurt by many church people in her career as a minister, but she clung to her faith, and to her church, all the same. It has taken her years to process through some of that grief, but she has come out resilient, knowing that the persecution she faced from within and without served the purpose of loving others well through their own grief and teaching her that rising from suffering is just practice for rising from the dead.

And that's what your pain may do for you too: teach you, mold you, and even love you. It may be hard to see it from where you are, but your pain from the church may be the very thing that draws you back in, not to experience it all over again, but to process it, to deal with it, and to face it head-on. In doing so, you will rehearse your resurrection, which is the whole point of the Christian faith.

We don't know where you are on your grief journey from leaving the church, or even if you think you're on one at all. You may think this is all hogwash. We get that. We thought that at one point too. But what we do know is that you can't just vacuum out a major portion of a person's life without there being a significant process of change. We're calling that grief because it most neatly maps onto what therapists have observed in dealing with death, loss, and other tragedies. In the same way, we believe that you must process your pain. Our goal in helping you do that is not to convince you to go back to church. Maybe you will. Maybe you won't. Rather, we hope that you will do something positive with the situation you're in and that maybe, just maybe, you'll bloom where you're planted.

Further Questions

1. What has been your experience with the church? Take some time to detail your journey in all its ups and downs.
2. What major influences caused you to be where you are on your faith/church journey? If you've left faith or church, why? If not, why not?
3. If you left faith or church, what stage or stages of grieving that loss have you gone through? What was that experience like?
4. If you haven't left faith or church, how have you processed any pain or trauma you might have received there?

2

That's in the Bible?

You might not have noticed that the Old Testament book of Psalms is actually five books. Just take a look at the beginnings of Psalms 1, 42, 73, 90, and 107. Each one has a marker at the top indicating that it introduces a new book. Why do these books exist this way? Scholars tend to settle on two key reasons. The first is the scroll length. Putting all 150 psalms together on one scroll would have been far too long for general copying purposes, so they cut it into sections. Psalms isn't the only book to do this, as we still have some of these divisions today in the forms of 1 and 2 Samuel, 1 and 2 Kings, 1 and 2 Chronicles, and Ezra-Nehemiah. Those weren't separate works in their original writings, but they were divided by later editors for thematic purposes or for the sake of the scribes so their scrolls wouldn't be too long.

The other reason the Psalms are likely divided into five sections is to match the five-book introduction to the Old Testament known as the Torah (the Law). This critical series of scriptures thoroughly defined the nation of Israel, and there are many references to it throughout the Psalms. So it only makes sense that, if they were going to divide the book, they would do it in fives.

We don't tell you that just to give you a history lesson, but also to introduce a point. If there's going to be a division in the text to divide it into sections, then we have to imagine it from the point of view of a reader with a scroll full of psalms. It wasn't like the book we have today, where we can just flip to our favorites. It was a scroll, so to get where you're going, you would always have to start at the top with whichever psalm was first and unroll the scroll to find the one you want. That makes the first psalm in each section special and important, so you'd think that each one would begin with magnificent praise to God and exaltation of his name.

Some of them do (Psalm 107, for example, for Book Five). But notably, one of the psalms that introduces its book, which carries the prominent place on the top of Book Three, is Psalm 73, a song of doubts about God.

It starts benignly enough: "Surely God is good to Israel, to those who are pure in heart" (v. 1). That sounds good. That sounds like we're about to talk about how great God is. "But," though, is the very next word. And it's on that word that we have to camp out for a bit. There's no special Hebrew word here, no clever parsing or wonky rendering. Every translation agrees. What are we supposed to do with that? We believe that we're meant to sit there for a moment and ponder. If God is good "to those who are pure in heart," what does that mean for us? Many of us trip over that phrase "pure in heart" because it requires us to ask ourselves the serious question of whether we fall into that category or not. If you spent any amount of time in church, your answer is probably no. The American church has been so good about proclaiming to us our broken sinfulness that you may have a gut reaction here to just say this doesn't apply to you. We get that. We live in that tension too. But notice how the author opens: "Surely, God is good to *Israel*" (emphasis ours). They can't all be pure in heart, right? This must, therefore, be a general statement.

This applies to all of us. Just replace "Israel" with "us": "Surely, God is good to [us], to those who are pure in heart."

"But," the author says, though. And it's here that we have to stop again and pay attention. This psalm was written by Asaph. That name doesn't exactly crack the Bible's Top Ten Most Famous list, so let's take a moment to remember who he is. Asaph worked with King David and King Solomon, the most important kings in Israel's history, at the peak of its spiritual and military might. David "appointed some of the Levites to minister before the ark of the LORD, to extol, thank, and praise the LORD, the God of Israel: Asaph was the chief" (1 Chronicles 16:4–5). So Asaph is the chief musical priest before the presence of God at his tabernacle and later his temple. This is about the holiest job you can imagine. This guy's actual, paying job was to lead others in singing to God daily at the most spiritually significant place in his whole nation. America doesn't really have an equivalent for this, so it's difficult to imagine. Try thinking of the conductor of the National Symphony Orchestra leading the band in the national anthem at the Capitol Building in Washington DC, on Independence Day, and you'll be near the mark. It's a solemn role full of significance, and that's exactly what Asaph is doing with his life.

So you'd think that this guy would be full of joy and bursting with praises for God. That's exactly how this psalm starts, after all. For thirteen words, anyway.

"But," Asaph continues, "as for me, my feet had almost slipped; I had nearly lost my foothold" (v. 2, emphasis ours). This is a moment of profound personal doubt. Asaph is utterly lost, sliding down the mountain of faith because he cannot find a foothold. The God he had placed his faith on was seemingly no longer there.

There's some debate about the translation of this verse. Some translators can't seem to stomach the implications of this, so it doesn't appear in most renderings, but one possible interpretation of the Hebrew here is "my steps *were caused* to slip" (emphasis ours, see the footnote in the *New American Standard Bible*). That has profound ramifications. The text doesn't say who or what caused the slipping, but we have learned from our experience and interviews that many people feel like it was God who caused those feet to slip. We were promised a "personal relationship with Jesus Christ," after all, and when we didn't get what appeared to be one, or when that relationship was corrupted by individual or corporate hypocrisy, many of us checked out. It felt like God had broken his word. But we argue that we should all keep reading.

"For I envied the arrogant when I saw the prosperity of the wicked" (v. 3). Make no mistake—the "wicked" Asaph describes often reside within the walls of Christendom. After all, who else could Asaph have been describing besides his fellow Israelites? He wasn't a soldier fighting the Philistines, and he didn't live on the outskirts of the land, interacting with foreigners very often. Instead, he was the highest musical minister and religious leader of his day, insulated well with other priests and high holy people. And as anyone who has been in a similar position can tell you, the "wicked" are often those right around you. It's the people who seem to get it easily, the people who spend their whole lives sinning but seem to get to experience God's presence, anyway. These people continue to receive grace after grace and blessing after blessing, despite living ruinous lives and sniping at you from a distance. These people get promoted up through the ranks of religion, even though they lack integrity and moral character. These people ruin faith for the rest of us, don't they?

Asaph seems to think so, for he continues.

> They have no struggles; their bodies are healthy and strong. They are free from common human burdens; they are not plagued by human ills. Therefore pride is their necklace; they clothe themselves with violence. From their callous hearts comes iniquity; their evil imaginations have no limits. They scoff, and speak with malice; with arrogance they threaten oppression. Their mouths lay claim to heaven, and

their tongues take possession of the earth. Therefore their people turn to them and drink up waters in abundance. They say, "How would God know? Does the Most High know anything?" This is what the wicked are like—always free of care, they go on amassing wealth. (vv. 4–12)

Asaph doesn't mince words. He hates these people. And that's what so many people feel toward their former churches and fellow Christians: hatred. But beneath that is another emotion, one that so easily entangles itself with that animosity: jealousy. Asaph even admits it in verse 2: "I *envied* the wicked" (emphasis ours). We think this is what drives many people out of the church. They (and we) see so many people so full of hypocrisy still getting socially advanced and seemingly blessed by God that they just can't stand it. These people go about without a care in the world, granted with a feast of faith that others never get a taste of. Their sweet belief comes so easily to them that it just appears saccharine to the rest of us. It can't possibly be real. Surely they must be faking it. Surely they must be hypocrites. And "surely in vain have I kept my heart pure and have washed my hands in innocence" (v. 13).

Isn't that what so many of us feel? Like all of our faith was vanity? We went to the camps and walked down the aisle. We went to church every Sunday and raised our hands and hearts in worship. We prayed and read our Bibles all the time. We spent time with God and with other Christians, just like we were supposed to. To paraphrase, we kept our hearts pure and washed our hands in innocence. And yet God was apparently nowhere to be found when people hurt us, slandered us, and maligned us. He wasn't there as our protection, as our rock and our shield as that other psalm promised (Psalm 18:2). Our most vital portions of ourselves, our very souls, were laid bare, only to be stomped upon.

Asaph reflects on this too, saying, "All day long I have been afflicted, and every morning brings new punishments. If I had spoken out like that, I would have betrayed your children" (Psalm 73:14–15). In other words, "God, I kept all your laws! I was kind and compassionate, full of love and grace. If I were half as mean as these other people, that would have been a betrayal of my principles. So why have I been so afflicted, God? Why?" Or, as Asaph says in the next verse, "When I tried to understand all this, it troubled me deeply" (v. 16). The word for "trouble" in Hebrew (*amal*) means "labor" or "toil," meaning that there was work to this. Asaph had to till the soil of his soul, yearning to comprehend, and he still may have found it dry.

It's here that we think Asaph stopped for a long time. He may have considered finishing the psalm on this sentence. It wouldn't have been the only lament among the psalms. He was well within his rights to end his work on this note, as are we. After all, he's going through the stages of grief. He's been through denial ("Surely, God is good to Israel"), anger ("I saw the prosperity of the wicked"), bargaining ("I envied the wicked"), and depression ("All day long I have been afflicted"). He's on his way toward acceptance and finding meaning. Surely he's done enough work for one day.

But Asaph doesn't stop there. He picks up his quill the next morning and continues his toil. He begins perhaps with a new note, a whole new movement in his song. Remember, many psalms were meant to be sung, and since Asaph was a musical minister, this was likely such a piece. So we like to imagine a key change at this point, for there's a momentous transition word, "until" (v. 17, NASB), meaning there's an ending to his suffering. There's a resolution to his pain and grief. "[Until] I entered the sanctuary of God" (v. 17), he says. Remember, Asaph gets to enter this sanctuary almost every day, so it's like he wrote the first part of this psalm the night before in the lonely midnight hours, only to rise the next morning, take it with him, and enter into the courts of God's Tabernacle. He may have read it once more before entering, making sure his words were right and his complaint clear.

But as soon as Asaph entered the Tabernacle, he wrote, "then I understood their final destiny" (v. 17), meaning the concluding prospect for the people who had hurt him. This may have been a reference to the end-times, but what's more likely is that this regards the futures of those who go on living like they always have, even in the presence of God. These are the people who go on hurting others, who attend his equivalent of church but do so causing pain to other people like Asaph. These are the people who ruined church for the rest of us, the ones responsible for our spiritual agony. What happens to these people? What is their "final destiny" (v. 17)?

"Surely you place them on slippery ground; you cast them down to ruin. How suddenly are they destroyed, completely swept away by terrors!" (vv. 18–19). This isn't necessarily a physical, literal punishment, but rather a representation that their faith is paper-thin because they place their hope in themselves and not in God. As much as they appear holy and righteous, their focus is on the opinions given by humans and not God, and so they have, as Jesus says, "received their reward in full" (Matthew 6:2, 5, 16). Asaph imagines this fall from grace as one that God himself causes. It's a reckoning for their arrogance. And notice, this isn't some corporeal destruction. Instead, they are "swept away by terrors" (v. 19), which are all in their head and heart. Another possible translation of the phrase *swept away* is *faded*. In other words, their memory will be all but gone. Their power over your heart will vanish in an instant when you enter the sanctuary of God.

That sanctuary doesn't have to be in a church. It can be the sanctuary of your soul as it encounters God. But you must enter it to witness this moment. When many people leave the church, the last thing they want to do is examine their spirit honestly. They'll do anything to avoid it. They may even become angry at us for even suggesting that they do so. But it's necessary. Asaph doesn't come to this revelation on his own, or even in his timing. It occurs to him when he enters God's presence. In his context, that meant the Tabernacle. In yours, it may simply be a quiet place where you honestly reflect on the condition of your heart for a while. Put your phone away. Shut off your internet. Set your smartwatch to charge. Even put this book down. Remove all distractions and think— really think—about where you are spiritually. Process your pain. Don't just ignore it. Deal with the emotions. Don't just brush them aside. Address the feelings. Don't just avoid them. Come into God's presence, even if you don't believe in him anymore, and dig deep within your soul. Get out a journal, and write down what comes to mind. Anything. Everything. All of what you're going through spiritually, no matter how it feels. Put a knife to your spirit, and carve out the gunk.

That's what Asaph had to do before he came to his realization. Before that, he was speaking without thinking. He even admits it. "When my heart was grieved and my spirit embittered, I was senseless and ignorant; I was a brute beast before you" (vv. 21–22). His emotions were raw, even animalistic. Before you get to the point where you can honestly address God, you may need to go through this process too. Yell at God. Scream at him. Emote directly in his face. Grieve unto him. He can take it. It's even in his Bible. Yes, we're seriously suggesting that you fight with God. After all, if it's a "personal relationship with Jesus," what is a good friendship if it's not been through this, if it's not been tested through trials?

You may not want that friendship. We get that. But we still think it's necessary to go through this process to grieve fully what you've lost. We believe that's the only way through to the better path. Even if all you want is for God to leave you alone and to have your spiritual agony voided for the rest of your life, you still have to go through this process. It's a breakup. It's a dissolution of a close relationship. That does not come without pain, no matter how much you want out.

But we hope that you'll keep reading what Asaph has to say. Because there's another big transition word coming up: "Yet," he continues, "I am always with you; you hold me by my right hand. You guide me with your counsel, and afterward you will take me into glory" (vv. 23–24). We don't think Asaph is necessarily talking about heaven here, but rather a sense of honor for having gone through this crisis of faith. Either way, after having endured this mess of emotions, Asaph is comforted by God, not directly through a personal revelation but by believing that God is ultimately good in the end. All Asaph has to do now is look to the sanctuary of God, the Tabernacle, or even his soul, and then he will know. The purpose of Asaph's pain was to reveal to him the goodness of God.

Maybe you have trouble believing that. We understand. We do too. Because we've gone through our own ordeals with the church, we know it can be hard to see God's virtue sometimes. But we place our hope, like Asaph, in the justice of a God who will one day sort out the people who tried their best to love him from the people who were just in it for the earthly power. Just because you left the church behind doesn't mean that God has left you behind. Not for one minute. That's why Asaph can say with confidence, "Whom have I in heaven but you? And earth has nothing I desire besides you. My flesh and my heart may fail, but God is the strength of my heart and my portion forever" (vv. 25–26).

See what he said there? It's okay for your flesh and heart to fail. It's okay for your soul to sorrow. It's even okay to quit. Because God doesn't quit. Where we fail, he succeeds. Where we don't have enough, he has an abundance. Where we are empty, he overflows. Where we are weak, he is strong. Forever.

Asaph continues, "Those who are far from you will perish; you destroy all who are unfaithful to you. But as for me, it is good to be near God. I have made the Sovereign LORD my refuge" (v. 27–28). That's all God asks of us: to draw near to him. Whatever that means for you, whatever that entails, it is good to draw near to God. It may hurt at first because of all the baggage you're still carrying from the pain you experienced at church. And you may never experience the personal presence of God. Asaph doesn't claim that. He only says that he is near God and that God is his refuge. God is a safe person to confide in, and he provides a safe place to be nurtured after you've been wounded, even if you were wounded by his people. God is not the church, nor is he bound by it. He loves it, he cares for it, but he is altogether separate from it. The church is made up of people, many of whom are bent on earthly power and self-advancement, but God is not a human, nor does he seek power for its own sake. He is "the compassionate and gracious God, slow to anger, abounding in love and faithfulness" (Exodus 34:6), and he will not leave you behind. He leaves the ninety-nine to chase after the one. He will not abandon his church, for he loves it, and in the same way, he will not abandon you, for he loves you.

Asaph doesn't quite end there. You'd think he'd be done, and perhaps he thought he was too. He's reached the acceptance phase. But there's one more stage to go through, finding meaning, and he gets there in the last sentence of this psalm. "I will tell of all your deeds" (v. 28), he says. It's in that sentence that we find what we must do to fully come to terms with what we've experienced. We must tell what God has done. It doesn't have to be to others at first. You can save face for a while. But you should at least start by telling yourself what God has done, proclaiming to your soul that God is still good. His church may have disappointed you, but he is still good. You may not have experienced him in the way the church suggested, but he is still good. You may have gone through immense pain because of the people who claimed God, but he is still good.

Even if you no longer believe in God, reflect on the relationship you used to have with him. Weren't there moments of immense grace? Wasn't there joy? Wasn't there peace, if only for a time? Be grateful for that, find meaning in that, even if it's no longer a part of your life, and even if it never will be again. Take a moment to thank God for that, even if you now think he's a meaningless fairy tale. Because he wasn't always such to you. Even if you've cast him out of your soul for good, surely there's still a place there for gratitude for what he used to mean to you.

We can all learn from Asaph that it's okay to doubt, even to remain in doubt for a long time. That's the middle ground we've been talking about. If Asaph, the holy music minister, can live there for a spell, then so can we. If the Bible is okay publishing this at the top of its scroll, then it's okay for this to be at the top of our minds. It's almost impossible to be honest with God without going through something like this. Very few people get through faith without a moment like it. It's not easy. It's advanced wholeheartedness. But it's so very necessary, if only to finish the process of grieving the loss of God and the church in your life. You may never come back to either, but if you can't find gratitude for what good you experienced, then we argue that you're not done. If you want to move beyond the church, then you have to forgive it. Otherwise, you're drinking poison for your soul, and you'll never be healed.

Further Questions

1. Read Psalm 73 on your own. What do you make of this psalm? How does it make you feel?

2. Have you ever felt like Asaph did at the beginning of the psalm, as if other people have it easier in faith than you do, even though they're sinful? What have you done with that feeling?

3. Have you come to any point of acceptance of your grief over the church? Have you discovered a meaning for your pain?

4. What does it mean to you for God to be a refuge and safe person with whom to share your agony from the church? Can you separate God from the church?

3

Orphans of God

B ut what if your beef is with God and not just the church? To answer that question, we ask another one that at first doesn't seem related, but we promise it is. What do you do when there's nothing you can do? We've all been there. This isn't a foreign concept. We've all, at some point, been in some place where we had no idea what to do next. We all want to be those people in movies and television shows who always seem to know just how to act in tough situations. They always have some awesome plan, and that plan always seems to work. They don't just bumble their way through challenges. No, they have a well-thought-out strategy for how to approach what's going on around them. But that's television. That's not real life. The truth is that most of us, at some point, maybe even often, have no idea what to do next. We feel like there's nothing we can do. And that presents a problem for us.

When Daniel was sixteen years old, he was driving to school. He was in Advanced Placement (AP) Chemistry, and this was the day of the big AP test. If you never took an AP class, the test at the end of the year is all that matters. You either pass it and get college credit, or you fail it and have to take that class over again in college. So this test was a big deal. Daniel's father was deployed at the time, so he was out of the house for a while. That meant that Daniel, at the mature age of sixteen, got to drive his dad's car. And this was perfect. He didn't have to be at school until late because the test didn't start first thing, so he got to sleep in and stroll in later. That was awesome. So there he was, driving to school like a stud in a puke brown Buick, thinking he was just the most fly guy because he was finally able to drive on his own.

Now, our hometown had a ton of back roads, and that's what he took to get to school. He didn't take the highway. Why? Because the back roads are more fun. They've got curves and hills and nobody on them. You can fly on the back roads. And that's exactly what this sixteen-year-old kid was doing.

But there was one problem. It had rained the night before, and those back roads, which were mostly in the shade, hadn't dried yet. So when Daniel came to one patch around a curve, he took it way too quickly and slid into a ditch. The very first thing that happened was that one of the tires blew. He didn't know why, but one of the tires was suddenly flat.

He got out of the car, wondering what to do. He looked around. Thankfully, there was no damage to the car. It was just a blown tire. That's no big deal, right? He'd changed a ton of tires in his life. He'd be a bit behind schedule, but he could still make it. He was thinking he was fine. This was Dad's car, after all, and Dad was one of the most over-prepared people in the world. Daniel opened up the trunk and started looking for what he needed. He saw the spare tire. Awesome. He was in business. But he quickly realized he had a really big problem. His father, Mr. Prepared, did not have a jack in his car. Then he was in real trouble because without a jack to lift the car, you can't change a tire.

He would have thought about a cell phone, except for one problem: He didn't have one at this stage of his life, so there was no way for him to call someone. So he started panicking, running around knocking on doors. The first door, no answer. The second door, no answer. The nearest house where someone opened the door was about a quarter-mile away. On foot. Thankfully, they were awake and home at 8:30 in the morning and were willing to help. And thankfully, they had a jack. It was a tiny little thing that he had no idea how to operate at first. But he was able to change his tire and got to his AP exam with exactly three minutes to spare, covered in dirt and tire muck. He had made it. And he aced that test too.

But for one panicked moment (maybe two), he had no idea what to do. He didn't have everything that he needed, which brought to mind that curious question: What do you do when there's nothing you can do? We all struggle when we run into a situation where there's no obvious solution. Being stuck stinks. When there's nothing to do but wait, and you can't do anything about it, all you can do is just sit there. And that is infuriating. It hurts. We gave a silly example of a blown tire. But there are more serious examples of this, aren't there? Like sitting in the waiting room, just biding time while the surgery is going on. There's nothing you can do. Not one thing. Or if you're trying to get pregnant and can't. You're doing everything right. You're following all the right methods. But it seems like there's nothing else you can do but wait. Or if you're working hard at your job and giving it all you've got, but it's going to be another three years before you're even eligible for a promotion. You're knocking it out of the park every day, but there's nothing left for you to do but wait. Being stuck stinks, and you don't always know what to do.

It's completely common to feel stuck in your relationship with God. It doesn't make you defective; it makes you human. Maybe you tried everything you could to fix it: You studied your Bible, prayed your knees down to the bone, changed your life, and corrected sinful patterns. You went to retreats and camps and conferences. You forged deep, meaningful relationships with Christians. And you serve others and rarely miss church. You've done it all. But you still feel alone in your relationship with God. You're still seeking God without ever feeling like you're finding him. You've still never had the personal relationship with Jesus Christ that Christians talk about. Can we all just be honest about that? Can we tell each other without fear that we feel that way? Does that make us less Christian? Less saved?

The Bible says that if "you seek the LORD your God, you will find him" (Deuteronomy 4:29). That's comforting. It's good to know that we'll find God if we seek him. But that's not the whole verse. Life would be so much easier if that were the whole verse. Life would be so much easier if finding God was a simple matter of looking for him. That's hopeful. We wish that were true. But it's not the whole verse. No, the rest of it reads like this: "If ... you seek the LORD your God, you will find him *if* you seek him with all your heart and with all your soul" (Deuteronomy 4:29, emphasis ours). And that straight-up scares us. Because now we have a reason to fear. Now we have a reason for it to be our fault.

So we try to fix it. We try everything. Reading the Bible. Meeting with Christian friends. Serving. Worshipping. Singing. Leading. Following. Praying. Meditating. Sitting and straining to hear God's voice. Repenting. Making lists of everything that's holding us back. We try and try to seek after God with all our hearts and with our souls. And you know what? We're exhausted. It doesn't even seem to work. We've been seeking and seeking and seeking and ... nothing. Nothing we can put our hands on and say it was a connection to God at that moment. It feels like the Bible isn't true, like God has broken his promises, and like we were sold a bad bill of goods. It feels like we've been lied to by the church and rejected by God.

We don't want to gloss over the pain of that reality because maybe that's you too. We imagine some Christians are reading this who are wondering if they even belong in church, or if we as authors have any business writing this book or leading in ministry if we feel this way. But all we're doing is humbly asking if there's anything we can do to reach out to God. It often doesn't feel like that. So we ask again: What do you do when there's nothing you can do?

Because the Bible is pretty clear on this issue. God says through both Hosea and Paul, "'I will have mercy on whom I will have mercy, and I will have compassion on whom I will have compassion.' It does not, therefore, depend on human desire or effort, but on God's mercy" (Romans 9:15–16). Now, there's a part of this that's comforting. One of the things we love about Christianity is that the problems of sin and eternal separation from God have already been resolved by Jesus. We're excited about that. We don't have to do anything. We don't have to keep trying to be perfect. Perfection has already been realized through Christ. We just have to believe in him. We love the fact that salvation does not depend on human desire or effort. That's good news.

But it's also kind of painful, isn't it? It seems to mean that there's nothing we can do to get closer to God and that a relationship with God depends entirely on him. What, then, do we do when we want a deeper, closer, more intimate relationship with God but he isn't, by any way we can tell, reaching out to us? Because it feels like if we can't point to some connection as a personal relationship with Jesus Christ, then we must not be God's people. We must be somehow outside of God's family. We must not be children of God. It feels like we're orphans. Not all of you are going to understand that. Some of you think that sounds a bit odd, and some of you think that's heretical, but we promise some people are reading this book who feel like that. It can't just be us.

Let us explain to you what it feels like so you can understand.

We're told we're saved by faith, but what happens when we run short of it? What happens when, after years of trying as we might, we simply go empty on faith? When we just have nothing left? Like the father of the demon-possessed child in the Bible, we've asked God to help us with our unbelief, but it doesn't seem like we've been helped. What little faith we've had has waned. We've been to church lots of times. We've gritted through hymns we didn't fully believe.

We've suffered through sermons that strained our reason. We've nearly torn our hair out in jealousy of the others who so obviously have connected with God because that's a gift we didn't receive. We've watched in grief as the Holy Spirit renders others unto tears of conviction and joy, but for us—we who bend our very wills like gymnasts to seek the face of God—we feel like we get nothing. It's the world's most disappointing game of peek-a-boo. God seems to hide the most from those who seek him the most.

People talk about having a relationship with God. We don't even know what that really means. How can we have a relationship with someone who never talks back? How can we love someone who doesn't even bother to call? Is our request too much for the Lord? We just want to see his face, to hear his voice, to feel his presence. He's done that for others. What made them worthy and us unworthy? David and Paul were both murderers, but God showed up for them. What gives? What will it take for us to feel like we're in a relationship with God? Because we would darken the very sun and so die just to witness God's light for an instant. But instead, we stand, it feels, in the cold night, outside the temple of God, banging on the door, begging to be let in, for just the hope of God in our lives.

That's what it feels like to be an orphan of God. Maybe that's not you, and that's okay. Maybe you've got a great relationship with God. That's wonderful. But please know that there are hurting souls around you who are reaching out to their heavenly Father with everything they have, but still feel like orphans. Christians, if you're close to God, if you've got that amazing relationship, you need to know that there are those of us who don't. And even though it might hurt you a little, we're going to ask something of you. We know you're in the warmth and mirth of God's presence. But for the sake of those around you, for the sake of the orphans, please be willing to step out into the cold with others. That sounds like a big ask. We're asking you to be open to doubt, pain, and what will feel like separation from God. But we orphans of God need you. We need you to stand out here with us.

Here's why you should do it: Because Jesus did. Jesus stepped out into the cold for us. Jesus stepped out of heaven, out of God's amazing presence, and it felt like he stepped out of God's love while he was on the cross. He even said that God, his Father, had forsaken him (Matthew 27:46). At that moment, Jesus, too, became an orphan of God—willingly. But he did it for us, all of us, who were all at one time orphans of God. He made you children, and you get to sit in God's lap. We're sure it's wonderful, but please come back for the rest of us. We need you. So just like Jesus did for you, please step back into the cold, and embrace someone who's in pain and who longs for the presence of God. You might just be the closest they ever get.

So you need to buy a coffee. You need to set aside some time. And you better come with more than cliches. We've heard them. We don't need answers. We need acknowledgment. We don't need easy outs. We need embracing. It's going to be hard for you, but we need you so badly. Please step out into the cold with us.

And for those of you out in the cold, one of the hardest things for you will be not resenting these Christians for that. You'll want them to leave. You'll want to push them away because you'll feel a distance between you and them. They, after all, have felt God. What do they know about where you are? That's what your instinct will tell you. But you've got to resist that instinct. Keep connecting with people who love God. Keep bringing them into your life. They may not ever be able to usher you into God's presence. Don't expect that. But they will give you hope, they'll guide you, and they'll keep you honest as you keep pursuing God. So when they offer you a coffee, take it. When they give you some time, spend it. And be patient and gracious when they say something you don't understand or think is just a platitude. It may very well be a life-giving truth. Think hard about what they tell you about seeking after God. After all, they've found him.

Whenever we as authors express this notion about being orphans of God, we get asked how it is that we remain Christian, how it is that we keep faith in a God we often feel wants very little to do with us. We don't have some highly memorable, three-point, alliterative answer to that question. If we did, we wouldn't be writing this. All we have is this: We don't always feel like we're God's people. We don't always feel like we're God's children. We don't often feel loved by God. We never have, and maybe never will, not on this earth, anyway. And we stare at verses like the one earlier from Romans. It reads, "It does not, therefore, depend on human desire or effort, but on God's mercy" (Romans 9:16). And that terrifies us some because it makes us feel like we can't do anything to fix it, that we'll be stuck as orphans of God forever.

But do you know what it says just a few verses later? This is God speaking. He says, "I will call them 'my people' who are not my people; and I will call her 'my loved one' who is not my loved one," and, "'In the very place where it was said to them, 'You are not my people,' there they will be called 'children of the living God'" (Romans 9:25–26). That's where we put our hope, in that even if we are orphans right now, God still wants us to be his children. Even if we don't feel loved right now, God still wants to love us. Even if we don't feel like we belong with God's people, God still wants us with him forever, for eternity.

You see, our hope is not built on our ability to perceive a relationship with Jesus Christ. Because then we would have no hope. Our hope is not built on our ability to feel a connection with Jesus. Because then we would have no hope. Our hope is not built on our ability to pursue God and commune with him. Because then we would have no hope. No, just like the old hymn says, "My hope is built on nothing less than Jesus' blood and righteousness. I shall not trust the sweetest frame but only lean on Jesus' name. On Christ the solid rock I stand. All other ground is sinking sand" (Edward Mote, "The Solid Rock").

A key phrase in there is "I shall not trust the sweetest frame." Here's what that means: It means that we can't build hope on our comfort. We can't build hope on our perceptions. We can't build hope on our efforts to pursue God. All that ground is sinking sand, but on Christ the solid rock we must stand. We must only lean on Jesus's name. And that's where our hope is. That's where your hope can be too, not on your apparent distance from God, not on your own efforts, but on the solid rock of Jesus, even when we can't feel him underneath us. By the grace of Jesus, we are no longer orphans. We may still feel like we are. We may still feel separated from God. But Christ has torn down the barriers between us and God. Christ has overcome the separation between God and us. Christ has sealed us for eternity in God's presence. Those who were not God's people are now God's people. Those who were not loved are now loved by God. Those who were not his children are now God's children. That includes us, and that includes you. That's the truth upon which our hope is built. That's the truth that brings us joy, even as we feel like we're still outside in the cold. That's what we hold onto.

Jesus said something on the night he was arrested. He was about to head straight to the cross and die for our sins, and he got one last chance to talk to his disciples. He had a lot to say, but he snuck this one thing in. It's often missed. Jesus wanted to make sure he told his disciples this before he was crucified. Watch this. "I will not leave you as orphans; I will come to you" (John 14:18). Jesus doesn't say you aren't an orphan. He says he won't leave you that way. Jesus doesn't say you won't feel abandoned. He says he won't leave you that way. Jesus doesn't say it won't seem like he isn't there. He says he won't leave you that way. Jesus says he will not leave you as an orphan. He will not leave you out in the cold. He will not leave you stranded. He will come to you. He came to us once, lived a perfect life, died on the cross, and was resurrected, all to adopt us as children of God. Jesus came to us once, and he will come to us again, that we should not be left as orphans.

Our fellow orphans, we don't have some great solution for you. We don't have all the answers. We don't have a gimmick or some magical formula to make it all better. We only have hope. A living hope, and that hope is Jesus. We can't claim to have some deep, intimate relationship with him. But we can claim to have hope in Jesus because he was resurrected from death back to life, and in just the same way, Jesus is resurrecting us. We can't see him now, and it doesn't always feel like he loves us. But he's proven that he loves us by sacrificing himself, and we cling to the cross of Christ. Our hope is built on nothing less than Jesus's blood and righteousness. Not on our ability, not on our perception, not on our effort, not even on our reaching out. No, on Christ the solid rock we stand. All other ground is sinking sand.

So what do you do when there's nothing you can do? You place your hope in Jesus.

Further Questions

1. Have you ever felt mad at God for not revealing himself to you? What did you do with that emotion?
2. What has been your experience with the phrase "personal relationship with Jesus Christ"? What does that mean to you? Has your understanding of it evolved?
3. Can you place your trust in a God you haven't experienced personally? How? Why?

4

The Jesus Who Walks Away

Pretty much all men reading this (and probably a lot of women) have some opinion on the following question: Who is the greatest NFL quarterback of all time? Many say Tom Brady, and as much as it may pain you to admit it, they're probably right. Some people might favor Brett Favre or Aaron Rodgers. Some might pick Patrick Mahomes. Some might even go back a ways and say John Elway or Joe Montana or Dan Marino. Maybe someone would go even further back and say Johnny Unitas or Bart Starr. A lot of you have an opinion on this. For us, though, there was only one answer to this question of the greatest quarterback ever: Peyton Manning.

Now, whether you agree with that or not is your problem. But certainly, he's in the top ten, right? He was a legend for nearly two decades, after all. After fourteen winning seasons with the Colts and two Super Bowls, though, the Colts decided to cut Manning in 2012 because of some injuries. After a season off and a ton of negotiations, Peyton eventually signed with the Denver Broncos. A lot of fans instantaneously gave up on the Colts and became Broncos fans. The first season there goes well, and boom! Peyton and the Broncos make the playoffs. They end up losing in double overtime to the Ravens. That's a painful loss, but you can't feel bad about it. The first season back, brand-new team, and it's a loss in double overtime; it's not like he was just killed out there. The first game of the next season? Manning throws seven touchdown passes against the same team. He was still amazing. He even broke the NFL record for touchdown passes that year, and his team scored an NFL record 606 points. They were going back to the playoffs, and all his fans were like, "Awww yeah … Super Bowl, here we come. We're about to watch our man, Peyton Manning, the greatest of all time, the sheriff himself, win another Super Bowl. It's going to be awesome."

The kickoff happens on February 2, 2014, at 6:02 p.m. exactly. Peyton Manning comes out. He sets up in the shotgun. He settles his feet. He looks left, he looks right. "Omaha! Omaha!" He signals with his knee. This is the good stuff. This is the drama. He steps forward. The ball is snapped. And it goes right over his head. Into the end zone for a safety.

Okay, okay. Bad start, Peyton, but you've got this. You're the greatest of all time. Come on now. You can do it. But then the other team scores. And Peyton's next drive is a three and out. And so is the next one. And the next one. Then Peyton throws a pick-six. We go to halftime, it's 22 to 0. The fans can't even enjoy Bruno Mars's halftime show; they're just trying to figure out how Peyton is going to make a huge comeback. They've seen him do it before. They know he's still in this. They've got it all plotted out in their head by the time the third quarter starts.

But after the second-half kickoff, the other team scores immediately. And Peyton still can't get his offense off the ground. It's late in the third quarter when Peyton finally puts a scoring drive together, but by then it's too late. The game is over. There's just not enough time. The greatest quarterback in the world, poised for the greatest comeback in history, loses. And he doesn't just lose. He loses badly: 43 to 8. It was a painful Super Bowl to watch for everyone. We're pretty sure most people went to bed after halftime. But it was especially painful for those who loved Peyton Manning.

After so much struggle and so much promise, Peyton just lost. He let everyone down. Now, don't feel too bad. Peyton did go on to one more Super Bowl two years later, won, and then promptly retired. That's the great ending we were all hoping for to begin with. But at that moment in 2014, a big hero fell.

This is very common. Our heroes fall all the time because they're human. Humans fail. Humans mess up. We're not perfect. That's not news. Putting someone on a pedestal is always dangerous. Now, you're reading a book about church, and you probably can guess what's coming. We just said that human beings are flawed, and they always let us down, and you're expecting us to say next that Jesus is perfect, and he, therefore, can't let us down. Right?

Wrong.

Jesus does let us down. He does it a lot.

And it's time that we're honest about that.

You see, we Christians are convinced that Jesus is all-loving and all-good and all-powerful, and that's true. Don't get us wrong. We're not saying that Jesus isn't those things. He is. It's just that we Christians read verses like "In all things God works for the good of those who love him" (Romans 8:28), and we think it means we have to deny all negative emotions about what's going on. We think that if God is good and is working for our good, we're not allowed to feel pain, anguish, loneliness, or abandonment. We think that because God works for our good in all things that we're supposed to feel good about all things. And so we deny our emotions. We act as if we're not allowed to feel certain ways toward Jesus. We shut down whole parts of our hearts, all in the name of faith.

And the way we know this is that when people are in pain, when something bad happens, when they hurt, one of the last places they want to go is the church. Right? Because when it comes to pain, church people can be the worst. It's already awkward when you're in pain and other people are experiencing joy. That usually just makes it feel worse, and you want to do anything but be open about it.

But even if you do open up, here's what tends to happen. You say, "I had a miscarriage."

And we church people often say, "God is good."

You say, "My husband cheated on me."

And we say, "God is good."

You say, "I lost my job."

And we say, "God is good."

You say, "My cancer is back."

And we say, "God is good."

Listen, if you're a church person, we get why you say that. We're church people too. If we're honest with ourselves, we don't say, "God is good," to make the other person feel better. We say, "God is good," to make ourselves feel better, to say something that sounds vaguely spiritual and feels faithful in a tough situation. Because it's not just that person's pain that hangs in the balance for us. It's our whole understanding of who God is. We cling to it, even at the expense of honesty. And so we try to shed some hope on their pain by showing them the long view of God's plan and how he makes all things work together for our good. That's not untrue. The Bible says that's true. We're not wrong in believing that. But we're also not helping by mentioning it right then, because it denies the validity of that person's pain. It denies them the right to feel.

We have written about Dr. Brené Brown before in other works. She's an expert on empathy. If you've not read her by now, do so. She speaks some good truth. She says that empathy and sympathy aren't the same thing. Empathy fuels connection, but sympathy fuels disconnection. Sympathy is trying to get people to feel about something in a particular way. Sympathy is trying to feel for people. Sympathy creates a distance between how someone feels and how we think they should feel. Empathy, however, is trying to feel with people. Empathy connects how someone else feels with how we feel.

Someone falls down a hole, see? And they say, "Hey, I'm stuck; it's dark. I'm overwhelmed."

Sympathy says to that person, "Ooh! It's bad down there. Don't worry. You'll get out. Believe. Pray hard." But sympathy stays out of the hole.

Empathy, on the other hand, jumps down into the hole with the other person. Empathy says, "I know what it's like down here because I'm here with you. And you're not alone."

It's a dangerous choice, a risky choice. Because to connect with you, we have to jump in that dark hole with you. We have to jump into doubt, pain, and shame with you. We have to connect with something inside ourselves, something vulnerable and agonizing, that knows that feeling, to sit with you in that hole. That's a risk, and it's not one we want to take. And that's why we say, "God is good." Not because that's true, even though it is, but because we don't want to jump down into that hole with you. It hurts too much.

So today, we're going to jump down into a hole. One you may be in. We're only going to make one promise, and it's this: For the problem we're about to present, we don't have a solution. We're not going to try to fix it. Our goal is to jump down into the hole of this problem with you and say, "Us too." So you know you're not alone. So you know you don't have to have it all figured out. So you know there's hope, even if it's only that you're not the only one.

Here's the hole we want to dive into today: feeling abandoned by Jesus. Now we Christians are awfully nice when it comes to Jesus. He's the Savior of the world. We believe that. Nothing we say here is going to deny that. But there are some of us—maybe many of us—who feel forsaken by Jesus. At times, we think it's his fault. At times, we think it's our fault. But most of the time, if you're anything like us, you do everything you can not to acknowledge this feeling.

Until it swells up out of nowhere. Until you can't sit through a worship song because you choke on the lyrics. Until your whole body wants to run out of the church because the sermon is about hope. Until you flip off Christian radio stations because you can't stand one more song celebrating how loving Jesus is. You've tried to experience Christ, you've tried to repent, you've tried to pray, you've tried to sing, and, if you're like us, you've tried to study, read, lead, and even preach, all to have Jesus in your life. Because you want what other people seem to have. You want that real relationship with God. But try as you might, it doesn't seem to you that God wants you back. And that hurts. It's empty and lonely. So you scream at the ceiling. You throw your Bible at a wall. You sin at the top of your lungs just to see if God cares. But still, at least most of the time, it seems like Jesus has just abandoned you.

If that's you, this chapter is for you. If that's not you, if you think you've got this whole Jesus thing figured out and you'll have unfailing hope forever, think again. If you're honest, you've experienced this at least once. If you haven't experienced it yet, there will be a point in your life when you feel like Jesus has left you in the dust. That's not us being defeatist. That's not us denying hope. That's us reading the Bible.

We know this because of the story in the Bible of a guy named John. Not John the disciple who wrote the Gospel of John. John the Baptist. He's not Baptist like Southern Baptist. He's Baptist in that he was famous for baptizing people, dunking them underwater as a symbol of spiritual change. John is the preacher who paved the way for Jesus's ministry. Many of Jesus's first followers were John's followers before. It was John who pointed to Jesus, who said that Jesus was the Savior of the world, and who baptized Jesus himself. John loved Jesus. And that love was not just one way. Jesus himself said, "Truly I tell you, among those born of women there has not risen anyone greater than John the Baptist" (Matthew 11:11). Jesus was saying that John the Baptist is the best man who ever lived. That's a huge compliment. We want Jesus to say that about us. Jesus clearly loved John.

So John loves Jesus, and Jesus loves John. There's no dispute about that. To John, Jesus is Peyton Manning. He's the best. He's his hero. But as we're going to see, John sees his Peyton Manning let him down, in a pretty major way.

You see, John got into some trouble. There was a ruler named Herod Antipas. Herod Antipas was married, but at some point in his marriage, he fell in love with another woman. Not just any woman, but a married woman. Not just any married woman, but his brother's wife. Not just his brother's wife, but also his niece. Now you know you're on the real Maury Povich. So Herod Antipas divorced his wife to marry his niece/sister-in-law. John the Baptist publicly criticized this. He said that was messed up.

Herod Antipas didn't like being criticized, so he threw John in prison. Now, a prison in those days wasn't like prison today. It was open-air, in the middle of the desert near a city called Machaerus. And John likely wasn't fed by his guards. His friends had to deliver food and water to him. So John probably went days at a time without food and water, much less sanitation or health care. It was desert torture as far as the eye could see. It must have seemed incredibly hopeless to John. By most accounts, John was likely in this desert prison for about a year and a half. We don't care how deep your relationship with Jesus goes, if you're in a desert prison with little food and little water, just baking in the sun day after day for a year and a half, you're going to start having doubts. You're going to say, "Hey, Jesus! What's with this? I thought you were the Messiah. I said you were going to save the world. How about starting with me?" John starts to mull, and he wonders if Jesus is who Jesus says he is. John is in the hole.

And it's the same hole that many of us are in. If we Christians are honest, it's the hole we're often in. It's the hole of feeling alone, of feeling like Jesus isn't there. Of feeling like you shout your soul to the heavens and hear nothing back but your own echo. And every time a pastor says that Jesus wants to have a personal relationship with you, you scoff. You fold your arms, you shake your head, and you think, *Really? When? I'm right here.* But it so often feels like Jesus is nowhere to be found.

John is in that hole, just like us. And just like us, he doubts. And this is something we want to make crystal clear: Doubt is not a sin. Doubt isn't even the opposite of faith. Doubt and faith aren't antonyms.

There are two rock climbers. They're both in a tricky situation. One reaches out to a rock above him and says, "I am certain this rock will hold me." The other reaches out and says, "I think this rock will hold me." Which climber is safe? Not the one who had more faith, but the one who reached for the right rock, regardless of how much faith he had in it.

Faith is not a feeling. It's an action. Faith is not living without doubt. Faith is reaching out even with your doubt. We'll say it again: God said to love him with everything we have. So if doubt is all we've got, doubt is what we'll love him with. John the Baptist is in the same place. He's in this prison. He's been there a while, waiting on his Savior to do some saving already, to get him out of the hole. Then John gets some news about Jesus.

"When Jesus heard that John had been put in prison, he withdrew to Galilee" (Matthew 4:12). Jesus *withdrew*. How many of us have ever had a moment when we felt like Jesus withdrew? Like he just wasn't even there. And notice what it says. Jesus didn't withdraw for no reason. "*When Jesus heard* that John had been put in prison, he withdrew" (emphasis ours). Not only did Jesus withdraw when John was put in prison, but because John was put in prison. That's just twisting the knife, right?

This is one of the ways we know the Bible tells the truth. If we were making up stories about Jesus, this is not the story we would make up. We would make Jesus come and rescue John. We would make Jesus be a hero to his beloved friend he cared about so much. But that doesn't happen. Jesus doesn't save the day here. Jesus lets John down. Jesus withdraws.

But wait, it gets even worse. "Leaving Nazareth, [Jesus] went and lived in Capernaum, which was by the lake" (Matthew 4:13). Now, that may not mean much to us right here. But that's over a hundred miles from where John is. And it's not just any hundred miles. John's in the desert, and Jesus is at the beach by a lake.

Church people, hear us out for a second. This is why our sympathy doesn't work. Those who are in pain, who feel abandoned by Jesus, who are in doubt and suffering and shame? They're in the desert prison. And we're talking to them from the lakeside beach. They're dying of thirst, and we're pointing to the bountiful water around us and saying, "Drink." But for them, where they are, a hundred miles away, there's no water. So when we say, "Drink," they reach for the sand because there's nothing else. That's why our sympathy feels so empty. That's why it doesn't work. Because we haven't taken the long, hundred-mile walk into the desert to suffer with them. We stay by our safe lake. We have water all around us, and we wonder why they don't just drink it.

When Lori's granddaughter (Daniel's niece) was four years old, she stayed with her for a couple of weeks. While she was staying with them, Lori gave the girl a toy. We don't quite remember what it was, but she loved this new toy. When she spoke to her mother on the phone that night, she talked all about it. She tried to express how much she liked it, but her mother was having trouble understanding what the toy did. The girl tried and tried to explain it, but couldn't find the right words. Finally, this girl, four years old and frustrated, said, "Just look at it, Mommy."

Of course, her mother couldn't look at it. Her mother was hundreds of miles away, talking to her daughter by phone. This girl, being four, couldn't share her experience with this toy with her mother because she couldn't make her mother see.

That's what it's like sometimes when people in pain talk to us Christians. We point to Jesus right next to us at the lake and say, "Look! There Jesus is. He's the Savior. He's the best. He wants a loving relationship with you." And we wonder why they don't see. It's because they're not at the lake. They're a hundred miles away in the desert. They can't see what we see. And we can't see what they see. Not unless *we* travel to them. So stop trying to sympathize. Stop trying to fix people's desert thirst by pointing to the oasis water next to you. Instead, go to them.

So John's been in prison for a while. He starts to have doubts about Jesus. When he first saw Jesus a year before, he unquestioningly said that Jesus was the Savior. He didn't have a single doubt. But after a year in prison, John has doubts. This tells us a crucial point. People in suffering, this is for you: The presence of doubt is not the absence of faith. If you're like us, you need to hear that pretty much every day. Having doubt doesn't mean your faith isn't real. John the Baptist was inspired directly by God to say Jesus was the Savior and saw with his own eyes God's presence descend from heaven onto Jesus as he baptized him. If he had doubts, we will too. That doesn't disqualify our faith, not in the slightest. Doubt is not the opposite of faith. John had doubts, and so can we.

Now the way we know John had doubts is that he sent some of his friends to talk to Jesus. "When John, who was in prison, heard about the deeds of the Messiah, he sent his disciples to ask him, 'Are you the one who is to come, or should we expect someone else?'" (Matthew 11:2–3). John's in prison, and he hears about all these great things Jesus is doing. But he still doubts if Jesus is the Savior. Jesus is doing all these amazing things. He's healing all these people. He's turning water into wine and whatnot. But John still doubts because John is still in the desert prison. He still doubts because he's still in the hole. He still doubts because he's still in pain.

This tells us another crucial thing: Seeing Jesus work in other people's lives doesn't necessarily give us hope for our own. John probably did not doubt that Jesus was doing great things. But that didn't give him full confidence that Jesus was his Savior. If anything, it made it worse. If we come to you with our pain, you pointing to how Jesus healed you may sound wonderful. But it creates a distance between us. It creates a contrast. Right then, we're not seeing the wonderful grace of Jesus in your life and having hope for ours. We're wondering why Jesus loves you more than he loves us. You thought you were providing us with hope, but we're left with despair. If we ask you for your story, by all means, share it, but when we're in pain, showing how Jesus has healed other people may not help. It might hurt worse.

And again scripture backs us up here. Jesus comes back to them. "Jesus replied, 'Go back and report to John what you hear and see: The blind receive sight, the lame walk, those who have leprosy are cleansed, the deaf hear, the dead are raised, and the good news is proclaimed to the poor'" (Matthew 11:4–5).

Now it sounds like Jesus just said something wonderful. But notice how it starts: "Go back" (v. 4). Jesus doesn't go himself. Jesus doesn't show up. No, Jesus sends these guys back to the desert to tell John in prison about all the wonderful things Jesus is doing for other people. If you're John, that's devastating. And Jesus knows it. Look at the next verse. Jesus lists all these things about what he's done for other people while John has been left in the prison to rot, and then Jesus says this. This is crucial. "Blessed is anyone who does not stumble on account of me" (Matthew 11:6).

Catch this. This is important. This could change your whole view of Jesus.

Jesus is saying that the natural response to his absence is to stumble. The natural response is to doubt. The natural response is to hurt and fear and despair. Anyone who tells you that God's seeming absence in your life is a test is lying. It's not a test. It's not a moment in which to simply have more faith, and you'll be fine. It's not that you've done something wrong. It's not that you're not saved. It's not your fault at all.

In this verse, Jesus admits his complicity in these feelings. Jesus says, "John, I know that what I'm doing right now hurts you. You're seeing me help everyone else right now and not you. You're completely justified in stumbling on account of me right now. I know you're hurting, and I know you're seeing me helping everybody else and not you. I feel your pain, and I understand your doubt. I'm in the hole with you. I'm in your desert prison with you, even as I stand in the oasis. I'm not going to deny you any of your emotions.

Your suffering is real, and I acknowledge it. You are completely justified in stumbling right now.

"But blessed are you if you don't."

That's the empathy of Jesus. Jesus doesn't fix the problem. John is still in prison. Jesus doesn't explain the problem away with some super churchy answer about the goodness of God. John is still in doubt. Jesus doesn't silver-line the problem by telling John to count his blessings. John is still in grief. Jesus doesn't sympathize with John. Jesus empathizes with John. Jesus doesn't look at John's pain and say, "Buck up." He looks at John's pain and says, "Me too." He looks at John's pain and feels it with him.

And that's what Jesus does with us. Jesus sees our pain and feels it with us. Sometimes, he'll heal it. We see plenty of examples of that in the Bible. But sometimes, he won't. He didn't for John. That doesn't mean he's abandoned us or he doesn't love us or he's angry with us. On the contrary, Jesus loves us and feels our pain with us. As you go through the life of Jesus, you'll see that Jesus feels pain, just like us. He feels grief, just like us. He feels fear, anger, doubt, agony, and abandonment, just like us. Jesus is the ultimate empathizer, and he's the one sitting by the throne of God praying on our behalf. As the Bible says, "We do not have a [Jesus] who is unable to empathize with our weaknesses, but we have one who has been tempted in every way, just as we are—yet he did not sin" (Hebrews 4:15).

Jesus came down to earth to save the world, and that's what gives us joy and peace and hope. But he also came to live as one of us, to empathize with us, to connect with us. He doesn't expect your emotions and pains and doubts to just disappear. He expects to sit in them with you. That's because Jesus doesn't want censorship over you. He wants a relationship beside you. And that's where our hope comes from: the empathy of Jesus.

Further Questions

1. What has been your experience with pursuing Jesus? Has he always shown up? What was it like when he didn't?
2. What are some examples of sympathy versus empathy that you have experienced? How do you wish people had been there for you?
3. What does it mean to you to realize that Jesus doesn't always come through in the way we want? Does it cause you to stumble? How can you still move forward?

5

God the Promise-Breaker?

The world had collapsed. The stars had fallen from the skies. There was no food to eat, no water to drink, and no hope to be found. Not a single shred of dignity was left as people starved and parched to death and as the enemy's siege grew closer and closer. The line of King David had remained true for so long, but each successor had given himself over to idols and foreign alliances. Yahweh was a name that echoed from the distant past, shouted now only from the mouths of people who, at least at the time, seemed odd. Surely, God had abandoned Israel. Surely, Israel's God had been defeated.

For in the ninth year of Judah's King Zedekiah, Nebuchadnezzar of Babylon marched against Jerusalem and set up a siege so severe and so long lasting that all water dried up and all food went scarce. Then one day, the walls—both the representation and the substantiation of safety and prominence—the walls that had been there since time immemorial, came tumbling down. The Babylonian army rampaged through the streets like roaring lions, tearing people limb from limb.

And King Zedekiah, the man charged with protecting Jerusalem and all its inhabitants, the commander-in-chief himself, fled through the gate by his palace. Lines of Jewish exiles watched as their lord was chased through the night all the way to Jericho, his guards being picked off one by one by foreign archers. Finally at Jericho, the Babylonians caught up with Zedekiah and took him captive.

But they didn't kill him. Instead, they dragged him to Nebuchadnezzar, who held a drumhead trial and issued summary judgment against him before executing his sons one by one in front of him and then gouging out his eyes, ensuring that the last thing he saw was his own children being dashed to pieces and his royal line ending forever. They then bound the king in bronze shackles and dragged him off to exile in Babylon.

Less than a year later, the Babylonians tore down the city's walls stone by stone, set their holy temple ablaze, plundered their holiest artifacts, and burned the city to the ground. Jerusalem had fallen. Judah had fallen. God, it seemed, had fallen.

This was a time when all hope seemed lost and when the promises of God seemed forsaken. This story is obviously extreme, as we don't usually experience our king's eyes getting gouged out while his sons are murdered in front of him. But haven't we all been here? Haven't we all been in a moment when life came crashing down, when everything collapsed around us, and when the promises of God seemed completely broken? After all, God had promised to Abraham that his descendants would be a great nation. God had promised to Moses that the Israelites would be a kingdom of priests that changed the world. God had promised to David that his line would last forever. But all of those came tumbling down with each stone of Jerusalem's great wall.

If you ask most Christians about the promises of God, they'll tell you that they're absolute. They can't be broken. They're like the mountains, ever present and ever strong. Yet as Jesus once forecasted, even a mountain can be cast into the sea. And as he said that, he was standing on the mountain of God's temple. Thus, even the holiest of hills can be weathered down to nothing and thrown into the ocean. Even the mountains eventually die under the powers of wind, rain, and time.

Whether it's the promise of a child broken by miscarriage after miscarriage, the promise of purity shattered by rape or abuse, the promise of holy matrimony ripped asunder by adultery, the promise of career ministry dashed by accusations, the promise of a relationship with Jesus that was met with disappointing silence, or any number of other promises we thought God made to us that have been slammed against the rocks, we've all been here. For you, it may be a lifelong addiction or a seemingly eternal depression or a long, dark winter of the soul as your life falls apart around you. Whatever the case, you probably can resonate with the Israelites, who watched their whole world implode. Their account, however intense, is not an anomaly. Their story is our story.

What gives? Do the promises of God mean nothing? What does it mean that his covenants to Abraham, Moses, and David were all broken in the span of one year? More to the point, what does it mean to our everyday lives that God can fail to keep his promises to us? How do we live in that tension and yet cling to the faith that God is trustworthy? Can such a thing even be done?

Before you call us heretics, know that we are in good company asking these questions. Not only have many saints and sinners resounded with us, but the Bible itself also does, in the form of Psalm 89 by Ethan the Ezrahite. This psalm starts out innocently enough:

> I will sing of the LORD's great love forever; with my mouth I will make your faithfulness known through all generations. I will declare that your love stands firm forever, that you have established your faithfulness in heaven itself. (vv. 1–2)

Just by simple word repetition, we get the idea: God's faithfulness lasts forever. It supposedly endures on and on until time stops one day. This is a repeated biblical theme, starting all the way in Genesis before being explicitly stated in Exodus 34:6 and then demonstrated throughout Israel's story. This notion of God's faithfulness lasting forever is not a new concept to the psalmist here.

But it is a questioned concept, for from this point forward, Ethan recounts God's specific promises to King David, namely that God would keep a king on David's throne forever. Ethan talks about how God's creation represents his faithfulness too, and that even the skies and seas proclaim how enduring his promises are. On and on this goes for thirty-seven verses, until Ethan hits a hard stop.

> But you have rejected, you have spurned, you have
> been very angry with your anointed one. You have
> renounced the covenant with your servant and have
> defiled his crown in the dust. (vv. 38–39)

In other words, God seems to have broken his promise. After all, the last king's sons were killed in front of his eyes before he was carried off blind into exile. The royal line was cut off, and the seed of David lay fallow in the dirt, trampled under the feet of foreign soldiers led by an evil king. Not one whiff of hope remained. God, it appeared, had "renounced the covenant" (v. 39) forever. A covenant wasn't just any old promise. This wasn't like God not paying his mortgage. This was like God divorcing his way out of a marriage. This was supposed to have been forever, and Ethan thought God had clearly backed out.

This is the tension much of the American church simply doesn't recognize. So many of us were sold the notion of a personal relationship with Jesus Christ, only to be left out in the cold both by him and his church. We committed to God, giving over our whole lives and every ounce of our souls to him forever, but it kept looking to us as if God had backed out of his end of the promise. Prayers didn't just get answered with a no; they didn't get answered at all. Cries at the ceiling and into the night went ignored. Tears were regarded as drivel. The crowns we were promised as saints of the Lord Most High were, as Ethan put it, "defiled in the dust" (v. 39). Alongside Ethan, we cry out, "How long, LORD? Will you hide yourself forever? How long will your wrath burn like fire? Remember how fleeting is my life. For what futility you have created all humanity!" (vv. 46–47).

Forever, he says. That's the same word he used about God's promises, that they, too, lasted eternally. But apparently so does his anger, and it's this anger that many post-Christians feel from God and from the church. Yes, God's wrath is on full display in the scriptures, and yes, that wrath is tragically misunderstood both by Christians and their enemies. But that's not why people think God is angry at them. They think that because of personal experience, not scriptural explanation. The Bible only seems to back up what they already feel, that God has abandoned them forever, even though his promises were supposed to be forever. They think God is angry at them because a pastor yelled at them, a parent abandoned them, or a friend or mentor abused their trust. These people became God's representatives in their mind, and if they could not find their way to loving them well, then how could God?

This isn't an original story. We have heard it over and over again from people across all spectrums of faith. This is the kid who goes to church every Sunday, only to be bullied there by the teachers who can't stand all their questions. This is the teenager who desperately seeks spiritual mentorship, only to be shut down by every potential mentor he meets. This is the career minister who gets stabbed in the back by her coworker at the church. This is the guy who calls out the pastor for making a mean-spirited joke from the pulpit, only to be yelled at and drummed out of the church himself.

Those are all true stories. Each made it seem like God was too high up and too far away, that the covenants of God weren't eternal at all, just the fleeting promises of fleeting men. Ten times Ethan reminds God of his divine faithfulness (vv. 1, 2, 5, 8, 14, 19, 24, 33, 37, 49), and eight times Ethan uses the word *forever* to describe a character trait of God (vv. 1, 2, 4, 28, 29, 36, 37, 46). But each time, we imagine Ethan's ink being blotted with tears. Every time he wrote the word *faithful*, he must have thought how faithless was the God who would rob Jerusalem of its king. Each time he wrote the word *forever*, he must have remembered the burning ashes of God's temple being razed to the ground.

Every Sunday morning, we can sing those famous words, "His love endures forever," from Psalm 136, but with each repetition, there echoes a tinge of doubt, and with each fresh taste of hell in our mouths, that doubt grows. We ask the same question as Ethan:

> Lord, where is your former great love, which in your
> faithfulness you swore to David? (Psalm 89:49)

God, where did you go? You ran great guns in the beginning. It was a sight to see. You wrote your name in the skies and defeated our enemies right before our eyes. Sins burned like parchment before you, and you made us holy. We committed our whole selves to you forever, knowing that you had done the same for us. We wrapped our lives and bodies around worshipping you, and you gave us your very Spirit. But where did that Spirit run off to? You told us we were temples and that your presence would be with us, so where is it? We who reach out in the night for you, what about us?

What's so interesting about this psalm is that it almost ends on that note. But for verse 52, the whole psalm would be about how God had broken his promise. But then, Ethan opens up in a resounding and bold acclamation:

> Praise be to the LORD forever! Amen and Amen.
> (v. 52)

There's that word *forever* again, appearing for the ninth time in this psalm. Only this time, it doesn't describe God but rather a response to God, shouting out with all Ethan's soul that even though

God had seemingly broken his promise, he still believed the Lord would come through in the end. What's even more interesting is that word *Amen* being used twice. It's one of those churchy words that we all use in Christianese, but none of us really knows what it means. It comes from a Hebrew root (*aman*), which usually gets translated as—don't miss this—"faithful." That word's root gets repeated all throughout Psalm 89, over and over again. At first, it describes God's actions toward us, but here, at the very end, it describes, perhaps, our actions toward God. Thus, Ethan, even in his darkest moment of doubting God's goodness and faithfulness, pledges his fidelity to a God he can barely comprehend in that moment.

This opens up all sorts of new possibilities for us. Apparently, it's biblically sanctioned to openly doubt God's faithfulness to his covenantal promises. Since the Bible expresses it so clearly, we ought also to have that right. It's not inappropriate to do so. Ethan's laments are the holy words of scripture: "God-breathed and ... useful for teaching, rebuking, correcting, and training in righteousness, so that the servant of God may be thoroughly equipped for every good work" (2 Timothy 3:16–17). That means we're supposed to learn from this psalm instructively. Evidently, it's good and righteous for us to question God's faithfulness. Don't let anyone tell you otherwise. Doubting God's loyal love isn't a sin any more than doubting your parents makes you a bad child. It's part of any real relationship to go through periods of questioning, even distrust and suspicion, such as Ethan experienced here.

But notice that word *praise* in this verse. The Hebrew word is *barak*, meaning "blessing." Again, that's a fairly religious word without a lot of unchurchy references. Usually when we bless someone, it's because they've sneezed. But in the biblical context, it means to raise up or salute. In the rich history of the Hebrew scriptures, it harkens back to the early chapters of Genesis, where God blesses Adam and Eve as rulers of his good world (1:28), then Noah and his family to fill the earth (9:1), and then finally Abraham, through whom God plans to rescue the nations (12:2–3).

By repeating this word in Psalm 89, Ethan is reminding himself and his audience that God has blessed us all from the very beginning and that even when he seems far off, he is right at hand.

Thus in his last breathless words, having fully expressed his grief and sorrow, Ethan echoes back to God what the Lord originally boomed from the skies: blessings. Blessings forever. Faithfulness and faithfulness. Amen and amen. It's the last hope of the last exile of the last city of Israel.

And that hope was not in vain. As the story goes in 2 Kings 25, one of royal blood was left alive and declared the ruler of what was left of the exiles of Judah, King Jehoiachin. And when the next king of Babylon rose to power,

> he released Jehoiachin king of Judah from prison. ...
> He spoke kindly to him and gave him a seat of honor
> higher than those of the other kings who were with
> him in Babylon. So Jehoiachin put aside his prison
> clothes and for the rest of his life ate regularly at the
> king's table. Day by day the king gave Jehoiachin
> a regular allowance as long as he lived. (vv. 27–30)

That cliffhanger is how the story of the book of 2 Kings ends. The Israelites are in exile, their homeland is destroyed, their capital lies in ruins, and their frail king is captive. But there's hope. Even in this wretched estate, God is still blessing the line of David "higher than ... the other kings who were with him" (v. 28), winking at us from on high that God's not done with his covenants with Abraham, Moses, or David. God's not done by a long shot.

Thus, we resonate with the hope of Ethan the psalmist. But that's not a shallow hope. It's precisely because Ethan embraces the full force of lamentation that we can even begin to understand his praise. He doesn't skirt the issue or try to defend God's honor, like so many Christians do. Rather, he tells God exactly what he feels and how he experiences what looks like a broken promise.

What do we learn from all this? How does Psalm 89 apply to our lives and to this conversation on those who have left the American church? Well, by many accounts, the American church has broken the promises it made. Promises like safety, reconciliation, and forgiveness. And since it proclaims it is an extension of God, it makes it seem like he has broken those promises as well. When many people left church, their lives were fundamentally altered. They lost friendships, mentorships, even family relationships, and sometimes marriages and children. They feel like they lost Jesus, whom they loved so much. They think God is angry with them, that his wrath rests on them for their decision to leave, and that the city of their faith has been invaded and burned to the ground. They feel like Ethan the Ezrahite, and many, in the dark night, take their lament straight to God himself.

And it's in that moment that they become the most like Jesus. Jesus cried out from the cross, "My God, my God, why have you forsaken me?" (Matthew 27:46, Mark 15:34). He was a man well acquainted with this feeling of abandonment. It must have seemed for him at that moment that God had broken all his promises, that the resonances of heaven that celebrated his birth and baptism were hollow gestures, and that he wasn't really the Son of God as he had been told. The separation of Jesus from his Father on that hill is palpable and devastating—and hopeful.

It's hopeful because Jesus, being the Son of God and "full of the Holy Spirit" (Luke 4:1), still felt the same separation as Ethan and as us. We are not alone in our grief at the loss of a Father or at the apparent breaking of his promise. If Jesus felt that separation and yet prevailed, then so can we. We can live into this tension by his strength and wisdom, echoing with both Jesus and Ethan when they both cry out, "How long, LORD?" (Psalm 89:46) and "Praise be to the LORD forever. Amen and Amen" (v. 52).

The application of this may not be immediately evident to you. That's okay. Maybe you still feel like God has broken, and continues to break, his promises to you. We've certainly been there ourselves.

To some extent, that thought crosses our minds every day, or at least every week. But if we can bring ourselves to the full measure of our emotions about it, if we can fully express what it is that we're experiencing, the answer from the heavens isn't just a still, small voice. It's a body on a cross, bleeding and broken for us, shouting right alongside us our grief, our lament, and in the end, our praise.

Further Questions

1. What promises do you feel God has made to you? How has he lived up to those promises over the course of your life?

2. What significance does it have to you to learn that the Bible expresses laments of doubt about God's promises? How does that make you feel?

3. What would it take for you to move from grief about seemingly broken promises to praising God forever, like Ethan does in Psalm 89:52? What emotional, mental, or spiritual hurdles lie in the way? How can you overcome them like Ethan did?

6

Why You (Probably) Didn't Get a
Personal Relationship with Jesus

For some people, though, what we've described so far isn't good news. That's what we Christians call the whole Jesus movement—good news, or *Gospel*—but for many, it simply feels like noise. After all, they (and we, at many times) tried to find God and instead got silence. We strained to believe the incredulity of a crucified and resurrected Jesus, but in the end, our cynical souls won out. What does that mean for us? How do we move forward in a way that honors our traditions and faith, and yet stands up to reasonable doubt?

One way, we think, is by melting down our idols and transforming them into the holy objects of God. Now, that sentence probably falls on a lot of deaf ears because it involves a metaphor couched in tens of thousands of years of human history, all while the modern era has ignored that history and moved humanity forward. That's all good stuff. We're glad that very few Americans physically bow down and worship objects of stone, wood, or gold any more. Granted, we've traded that idolatry for a worship of vague "forces," like money, sex, and power. But still, progress.

But let's take a look instead at the ancient practice of idol worship. In the Bible, we're first introduced to it in Genesis 31, when Jacob's wife, Rachel, steals her father's household idols on their way out the door and hides them under herself by pretending she's menstruating. But that strange story only hints at what's to come later for God's people, the Israelites. After he raised them up out of Egypt with the ten plagues and the splitting of the Sea of Reeds, delivering them from Pharaoh and the greatest empire of their day, the Israelites arrived at Mount Sinai to enter into a covenant with God. This is something like a marriage, but it's more contractual. God said that he would be with the Israelites and become their strong warrior forever in their promised land if they would commit themselves to him alone and become a "kingdom of priests" (Exodus 19:6) to rescue the world from its own evil. The Israelites heartily agreed to this arrangement, shouting together, "Everything the LORD has said we will do" (Exodus 24:3).

Then something strange happens. Moses, the deliverer of this covenant promise from God, disappears "on the mountain for forty days and forty nights" (v. 18). Over the next few chapters, we the audience are let into what happens, as God helps Moses prepare for God's presence to dwell among his people forever in what will be known as the tabernacle, a mobile hotspot of his Holy Spirit. But the Israelites are just left outside the cloud of God's presence, made to wait in the desert by the mountainside for over a month. Even though God's physical manifestation is right above them, he starts to feel eerily distant.

This is where most of us arrive at some point in our lives. God showed up, did big miraculous things, totally blew our minds, and then, in a whiff, seemed to disappear for a long, dreadful silence. It's the camp where we feel we met Jesus almost face to face, only to slog back home and think of it all as an emotional pressure cooker instead of a divine theophany. It's the church service where we witness ourselves and others elevated to great spiritual heights, only to see those people (and ourselves) still contribute to evil in the world later on. It's the testimony we hear and experience as people defeat addictions, overcome sins, and choose righteousness, only to find out that they were still feeble, or even lying the whole time. Nearly every person who has made some claim to Christianity has at some point felt close to God, as if a covenant of old had been made, but then it seemed like he hid his face and darkened out the sun to conceal his holy presence. We lament how temporary and fleeting is the Spirit of God, how unpredictable and unmanageable. Perhaps we had better place our trust in something more tameable.

That's exactly what the Israelites did. Even with God's magnificent cloud right next to them on the mountain, they grumble to Aaron the high priest, saying, "Come, make us gods who will go before us. As for this fellow Moses who brought us up out of Egypt, we don't know what has happened to him" (Exodus 32:1). This initially sounds foreign to us. Why would they need an idol to lead them when they can just walk away on their own? But pause here for a moment. Isn't this what we do? When God doesn't show up in our lives the way we want, don't we also select another god to follow? Whether that's money, prestige, power, pleasure, or comfort, we all try to get the benefits of having a good god without the difficulty of worshipping the one true God. Because, as it turns out, he's not tameable or manageable at all. He is the "consuming fire on top of the mountain" (Exodus 24:17), outside the control of any human influence and totally without hindrance. It is only his good character that prevents him from swallowing up the whole world in his awesome power. He is not a genie in a bottle; he is the singular deity on high. As a later prophet would remark, "Who of us can dwell with the consuming fire? Who of us can dwell with everlasting burning?" (Isaiah 33:14).

Many of us live in this tension too. We want all the dependable advantages of God but none of his alarming magnificence. So we, like the Israelites, give up on this unpredictable God we cannot regulate, and we choose to make new gods, even ones we know aren't real or satisfying. The Israelites' ploy to make a controllable god is fairly obvious in the text. When Aaron collects their offerings from them and creates the famous golden calf, he says, "These are your gods, Israel, who brought you up out of Egypt" (Exodus 32:4) and proclaims "a festival to the LORD" (v. 5), invoking God's holiest name as the appellation for the idol he created.

We do this too. We call the foolish pursuits of this world blessings, as if they come from God, so we can all get what we really want instead of pursuing a meaningful relationship with the creator. He is beyond our control and imagination, so we create things within our control and imagination, and name them God. This is what happens when we chase after that promotion but blame God when we don't get it, or when we lust after that one person we fancy but accuse God of denying us when they rebuff our affections. When things go our way, we're selfish with the credit. When they don't, we're generous with the blame, particularly on a divine scale. We want a predictable, manageable God to go before us.

But that is not the God we have. We worship a wild and untameable God.

The reason we bring up this story is because it gives us an excuse to bring up another, seemingly unrelated, story in Exodus. It's a story most people skip because it's about the building of the tabernacle, and it goes into some detail about the materials necessary to create it. What gets missed, though, is how different the true God is from the false idol the Israelites made. In the golden calf narrative, Aaron commanded the Israelites to "take off the gold earrings that your wives, your sons and your daughters are wearing, and bring them to me" (Exodus 32:2) so that he could use them to forge the idol. But when God finally forgives the Israelites (which he does in the span of just one chapter), he also takes up an offering for his holy artifacts inside the tabernacle, saying, "Everyone who is *willing* is to bring to the Lord an offering" (Exodus 35:5, emphasis ours).

Whereas Aaron took advantage of the people's impatience and ordered them to give up their gold, God only accepts an offering from those who have what other translations call "a willing heart" (v. 5, NASB). That word for *heart* is used ten times in this section, a coincidence harkening back to the famous Ten Commandments that we believe should not be overlooked, for here we have a God who does not levy a tax on people who can't afford it or even on those who are unwilling, but only on those who desire to love God back the way he has loved them. Remember, the tabernacle is going to be the hotspot of God's presence for the Israelites for centuries to come. It's the mobile spirit-house of Yahweh. Thus, the people who are investing in this are committing themselves to a future with a God they know they can't control but whom they love and submit to, anyway. They are renewing the covenant by giving up the things that gave them wealth, power, and prestige, with some of the same materials they had previously used to make the golden calf.

That's why the original word here for *willing* is also the Hebrew word for "princely." Their cheerful giving commits them to a relationship wherein they will be called God's "firstborn son" (Exodus 4:22), what one New Testament author would call "a royal priesthood" (1 Peter 2:9). When these Israelites offer up their possessions, they're not just giving away money. They're choosing to chase after God with all they have. As Jesus would later comment, "Where your treasure is, there your heart will be also" (Matthew 6:21). In this moment, the Israelites are placing their hearts in the storehouse of God, even though he is beyond their capacity to understand or imagine, all because they want a relationship with him.

What should get noticed here is that most of the offerings given by the Israelites were used to make holy artifacts inside the tabernacle, particularly in the Holy Place and the Holy of Holies, where only priests and the high priest could go, respectively, and even then only on special occasions after performing special rituals. Therefore, the people have given up gold and other possessions as a freewill offering to reinforce a relationship they would never themselves experience, as most are not Levites or priests. The sacrifice they are making will ensure a connection they will never enjoy, except by proxy.

We can all learn from this unique act of sacrifice. Many people (ourselves included) were pitched the idea that the Christian faith was, to some degree, about us as individuals. It was called a personal relationship with Jesus Christ. Individual activities such as prayer, meditation, and Bible reading were encouraged most heavily. A person's spiritual growth was the utmost goal. That was the primary message of American Christianity for over fifty years, and many churches still reinforce it to this day.

But it's simply untrue, at least partially. While that relationship is wonderful, and while those individual activities are good disciplines to have, and while your maturity would be a wonderful outcome, those are not the essence of Christianity. It's not primarily about personal salvation or individual faith, although those are great results. Christianity is, rather, a community of people coming together in mutual sacrifice and love to bring about the reconciliation of the world to itself and, more importantly, of heaven to earth. The famous prayer of Jesus isn't, "Please save me from hell and make me a good person." Instead, it's "Your kingdom come, your will be done, on earth as it is in heaven" (Matthew 6:10). That prayer does ask for forgiveness from sins, but it immediately contextualizes that forgiveness in relationship to others: "Forgive us our debts, as we also have forgiven our debtors" (v. 12).

That's exactly what those bringing offerings were doing in Exodus 35. They were giving up things that mattered to them a great deal, not just expensive things but also their own skills and talents (see v. 10), to bring about a reality that wasn't just about them or their individual relationship with God. Such a relationship barely entered into the mind of the average Jew, if it entered into it at all. God's covenant was not with one Israelite; it was with *all* Israel. The temple wasn't so the high priest could enter into the presence of God and bask in a personal relationship. It was so he, as

Israel's representative, could bring the whole nation into an accord with God. It was never about the individual; it was always about the community.

This is what the American breed of Christianity to which many of us were introduced got wrong, and what it generally still gets wrong. When you ask most Americans what our religion is all about, what they have heard is something along the lines of, "Believe that this Jesus fellow rose from the grave after being crucified, and do what he says, or else spend eternity in the bad place." From any biblical author's perspective, this is utter nonsense, and its dominance in American Christian thought is nothing short of groupthink, corporate delusion, and even rampant heresy. It has its roots in individualistic capitalism and Platonistic dualism, not the pages of the Bible. It's no wonder it has spread like a virus through our nation; it's tailor-made for the American dream, wherein you can project yourself onto streets of gold if you just try hard enough, believe the right things, and check all the right boxes.

But the God of the Bible knows what that is, and so do we if we stop long enough to hear what the silence is shouting at us. That's the golden calf, not the tabernacle. What God wants, what he's really after, is a relationship with a community, a covenant marriage with a holy people set apart for his mission to save the world. That's what he had in mind for Israel, and it's what he's still up to today with the church.

What's this got to do with you? Everything. We were all sold on the notion of an individual relationship with God, which sounds wonderful, but what if our salvation was never meant for us? What if we were supposed to use what God gave us to create holy spaces for other people to experience God? That's the next thing to happen in this chapter, after all. After everyone gives their "freewill offerings for all the work the LORD through Moses had commanded them to do" (Exodus 35:29), God appoints two men to craft the holy artifacts that will appear in the Holy Place and the Holy of Holies. They were "Bezalel ... of the tribe of Judah" (v. 30) and "Oholiab ...

of the tribe of Dan" (v. 34), which presents an interesting point. They weren't Levites and therefore weren't priests. They would use their craftsmanship to forge things that would serve other people's relationships with God. They would never be the high priest, or even a regular priest. Once they were done crafting the objects, they would never see them again. They were "filled ... with wisdom, with understanding, with knowledge and with all kinds of skills" (v. 31) to reinforce a communion they would never directly enjoy.

We think this is exactly what happens to many people. Only some people get a truly personal relationship with God, where they regularly experience his presence and commune with him. There are exceptions, of course, and those exceptions are often famous pastors and theologians. But notably, those acclaimed people become deeply influential in Christian thought and practice. They share their individual experience to forge a corporate relationship. The same thing happens in Exodus, where Bezalel and Oholiab are given "the ability to teach others" (v. 34) how to construct the artifacts, and those artifacts get used by the priests and high priest to make atonement for the Israelites before God. Nothing is sacredly individual or personal, but everything is communal and meant for the mutual benefit of all.

So the personal relationship with Jesus Christ that some people experience still isn't personal. It's for everybody. Yes, we're all walking temples of the Holy Spirit, and yes, we're all royal sons and daughters of God when we freely give up what we have for the sake of others. But we have to admit that the kind of relationship we thought we were supposed to get—with divine conversations and intimate interactions with God himself—is exceptionally rare. If that bothers you because you feel left outside in the cold, we get that. It bothers us too. Neither of us has ever had many particularly strong theophanic experiences (Lori one, Daniel none). And yeah, that hurts our feelings, because it seems, then, that God wants little to do with us.

But that's simply not true. Just because you (and we) don't get to hear a voice or feel a presence or palpably experience the Spirit doesn't mean that God loves us any less or that he loves the people with whom he blesses such things any more. Rather, we have what we have for the sake of the community. A particular pastor may have wonderful interactions with God regularly, and that may propel him or her to great heights of ministry. But Mother Teresa famously didn't have such interactions and even felt abandoned by God, and she had a greater impact on the world than most pastors ever will.

Individuals may be blessed with the enormous wonder of God, but they don't get to keep that for themselves. Their experience only makes sense in the context of the community covenant with God, and it is never solely theirs. In the same way, just because you've never had what they have doesn't mean you're not in the community and have nothing to contribute. You, too, have been filled "with the Spirit of God, with wisdom, with understanding, with knowledge and with all kinds of skills" (v. 31) in order to benefit the world and participate in the grander relationship with the divine. For some people, that's like Bezalel and Oholiab, where your talents get used to create long-lasting benefits for everyone; for others, it's the quiet encouragement you give sitting on a stoop to a person in agony reaching out for God. In any case, God's relationship is not with just one person. It's with all of us as a whole, and that's why it feels so mitigated to so many people. Because it was never about just you in the first place.

Paul discussed this in one of his letters. What we're about to say is one of those "life verses" that often gets ripped out of context, but worse than that, the translation takes some explanation for what we're about to say to make any sense. When Paul says "to offer your bodies as a living sacrifice, holy and pleasing to God" (Romans 12:1), we often think this is, again, about an individual's life. But notice what gets done here, even in English. *Bodies* is plural; *sacrifice* is singular. That's because the word here for *your* is talking about the collective.

When any one of us tries to make our lives a sacrifice to God, that's good, but when a whole community of believers gets together as one body to commit themselves to each other and to the world around them as a singular sacrifice, that's when something truly special occurs. It's when we come together and throw in our freewill offerings to God, both material and vocational, toward an allied goal that we can truly change the world, and "this is your true and proper worship" (v. 1). Not some amorphous, individual relationship with a tameable, personal deity, but a collective, powerful covenant with an almighty, all-consuming fire.

This is the best argument we can make for small groups and other highly communal church practices. Once you realize that Christ's bride is the whole, global church, you can't go on pretending that it's all about you. In a similar way, once you recognize that God is more interested in resolving the world's sins than just yours, you can—and must—think outside your own salvation and spiritual journey.

So the church needs to change its message. The good news doesn't only deal with an individual's relationship with God, an individual's eternal destiny, or even an individual's sin. Rather, it forges a new community of mutual love that together communes with God, seeks heaven's restoration with earth, and forgives the sins of the world. That's what Jesus was up to, and that's good news.

Further Questions

1. How have you tried to tame God to make him more manageable by you?
2. When did you first hear the phrase "personal relationship with Jesus Christ"? What did that mean to you at the time? What does it mean to you now?
3. What does it mean to you to learn that many people don't experience anything like a close, intimate relationship with God?
4. How can you learn from the story of Bezalel and Oholiab about how to contribute to the community instead of seeking a singular relationship with God?
5. How does it impact your understanding of the Gospel when you learn that it isn't about you as an individual? What does it mean to you now to be saved?

7

The Way of the Exile

Crash and Burn

So there are exiles from the church, orphans of God, an all-powerful deity who takes far too long to fulfill promises, and a Jesus who walks away. Those experiences are profound, but it might surprise you to know that it's not unique to you, nor even to our time. Plenty of God's people have felt that way before. There are whole sections of the Bible dedicated to this experience in the form of exile literature. If you remember your Bible history, you recall that Israel was chosen by God as his representative nation to the world, his "kingdom of priests" (Exodus 19:6). They were given a special set of instructions, known as the Torah, that was supposed to set them apart from the nations around them, and they were established by God as his holy people. But they did a rather horrible job of living up to this calling. From the very beginning, before the dust had even settled on their promised land, they lusted after idols, pursued selfish gains, and oppressed each other and others in bids for political and social power. There were some glimmers of righteousness under Joshua and later King David, but all in all, barring a few flirtations with God under later and lesser kings, Israel was a wholly corrupt nation, leading to disarray, injustices, and moral and military failure.

The prophets, God's spokespeople, began to speak out during this time. First, it was Obadiah proclaiming God's judgment against some of Israel's enemies, but soon that judgment would turn against Israel itself. As the later prophet Joel says, "Blow the trumpet in Zion [that is, Jerusalem]; sound the alarm on my holy hill. Let all who live in the land tremble, for the day of the LORD is coming. It is close at hand—a day of darkness and gloom, a day of clouds and blackness. Like dawn spreading across the mountains a large and mighty army comes, such as never was in ancient times nor ever will be in ages to come" (Joel 2:1–2). A major calamity was getting ready to come in the form of foreign armies and wars and even natural disasters. Gloom and agony were upon the Israelites from this day forward, as they had completely abandoned their God and continued along their downward spiral toward self-destruction.

Through these prophets, we get to see the heart of God. He longs for his people to love him back, but they simply refuse, over and over again. Like he says through his prophet Hosea, "My people are determined to turn from me. Even though they call me God Most High, I will by no means exalt them. How can I give you up, Ephraim? How can I hand you over, Israel? … My heart is changed within me; all my compassion is aroused" (Hosea 11:7–8). We see here the conflict God is having with himself. He desperately wants his people to return to him, but they are stiff-necked and stubborn. His compassion and love abound, but the Israelites are bent on ruin. They run away from God right into the waiting arms of sin, greed, power, lust, and pride.

Doesn't that sound familiar? Doesn't that remind us of the American church? Hasn't it done all these things? American Christians have chased after the wind too, pursuing money and material gain over the poor in spirit, loving political power more than spiritual health. But lest we become too haughty, doesn't that also remind us of ourselves? Aren't we all capable of this? Every one of us has fallen prey to this kind of idolatry and God-abandonment.

The American church is merely the focal point of that for most of us. Its hypocrisy as an institution exists because of our hypocrisy as individuals. We each individually contribute to the sin corporately. It's partially because of this collective commitment to self that the American church is losing its grip on reality and spiraling out of control. The church often laments individualism, but the truth is that much of its cultural sway is our fault. We were the ones who pitched that the relationship with Jesus was personal. We were the ones who made sin an individual crime and said that getting right with God was an individual choice instead of a collective one. None of that is necessarily untrue, but it's not the whole truth. Surely, there were some good people in Israel during the time of the prophets, but the nation as a whole sinned and thus found its way to destruction. In the same way, there are plenty of good people in the American church, but the collective whole has transgressed to such a degree that it is in danger of becoming like the Israel of old: corrupt, sold out, and powerless.

What happened to Israel? Eventually, their pattern became so self-destructive that they were utterly decimated (in the case of the Northern Kingdom) and exiled out of their homeland (in the case of the Southern Kingdom). The temple was plundered and burned to the ground, and the great city of Jerusalem had its walls torn down, one stone from another. This great calamity is recounted in several books of the Bible. Jeremiah recalls that Babylon "set fire to the temple of the LORD, the royal palace and all the houses of Jerusalem. Every important building [they] burned down. The whole Babylonian army, under the commander of the imperial guard, broke down all the walls around Jerusalem. Nebuzaradan, the commander of the guard, carried into exile some of the poorest people and those who remained in the city, along with the rest of the craftsmen and those who had deserted to the king of Babylon" (Jeremiah 52:13–16).

This was completely devastating. But did you catch something? Even for all the destruction, the Babylonians kept some alive. They did not fully wipe out the Israelites. No, they left behind a remnant. Like we said earlier, that's an important word in the Bible. Every time God brought down a calamity on the earth, he always left behind an intentional subset of people to carry his promise forward. First it was Noah after the Great Flood. Then, it was Moses being drawn from the water during Pharaoh's massacre of Israelite children. And then, after Israel's fall, a small number of them were left alive and with their culture somewhat intact. Like God said through his prophet, "I myself will gather the remnant of my flock out of all the countries where I have driven them and will bring them back to their pasture, where they will be fruitful and increase in number" (Jeremiah 23:3). This is God's promise to his people, that there will always be some left over after the disaster, whom God will call to return to him so they can be free and prosperous once more.

But that doesn't happen overnight. In the case of Israel, it took decades before any returned to their homeland, and they do not truly have self-governance over their holiest sites even to this day. So exile can take a long while. What should people do during it, then? How should they live if they have been exiled from their homeland, the religious environment they grew up in? And what does all this have to do with leaving the church?

The Two Options

If we're going to compare the American church's fall to ancient Israel's descent into destruction, then we must pay attention to how Israel fell and why. But more importantly, we must also be alert to what the leftovers after the exile had to say about their experience. For the most part, it seems like there are two primary options for how to respond to exile.

The first option is abandonment. Many Israelites chose this option and became full citizens of their captor nations by learning their language, taking on their idol gods, and completely forgetting about their prior relationship with God. This wasn't too hard of a choice. They had already all but abandoned God to begin with. It's too easy to put God by the wayside when he doesn't mean much to you, anyway. Thus, many Israelites simply became Babylonians or Assyrians or Greeks, keeping only the broadest strokes of their ethnic and religious ties alive (circumcision being a key one, although even that fell by the wayside for many former Israelites). When asked, they might not even think to call themselves Israelites before they declared their allegiance to the nation that had captured them.

Many former churchgoers do this too. It's not at all uncommon for people who have left the church to leave all sense of Christian practice behind. They take their Bibles off the shelf for good. They stop praying. They abandon all Christian gatherings and activities. They give up on any prior notions of sexual or moral purity. And when asked, they refer to themselves as unaffiliated when it comes to religious ties. They won't necessarily go quite as far as calling themselves atheists or agnostics, but for all intents and purposes, they are no longer any kind of Christian. In fact, they are no longer of any religion whatsoever, even the denial of religion. They are just *none of the above.* They barely have a name when it comes to their faith, and their religious identity has all but disappeared.

Such was the case with many Israelites. They had simply adopted roles in their respective overlords' kingdoms, largely not questioning the customs and moral practices of their new homes. Esther in particular gave up on sexual moral purity to secure her position as queen, and Nehemiah would almost certainly have eaten food sacrificed to idols as one of the king's cupbearers and food-tasters. Questions of conscience didn't possess their minds very much. But when opportunities presented themselves, they made great attempts to restore some of Israel's fate. Esther saved the Jewish people from genocide by appealing to the king, and Nehemiah led a project to rebuild the walls of Jerusalem, for example. But still, for most of their lives before those events, they simply abandoned their former status as Israelites.

This doesn't translate neatly into today's scenario, but one example does come to mind. Though many people claim to be unaffiliated when asked about their religious preference, a large contingent of non-church people still call themselves Christian when push comes to shove. This willingness to still identify with their religious heritage indicates some level of connection with the church, even if only in name. These people barely practice their Christianity, if at all, perhaps only attending at Christmas or Easter, but many make the claim of trying to live good lives based on their Christian upbringing. As we said, this isn't a neat parallel, but it does provide some context into what people are experiencing that's like what the exiled Israelites went through. There was a remnant, but they had religiously checked out.

The second option many Israelites took was revolt. They simply would not give in to the pressures of their new environments, so they took to military defiance. Such was the case with the Maccabees, of whom the American church remembers little because most of us don't include their texts in our Bibles. To bring you up to speed, here's the story: In 167 BCE, when King Antiochus IV Epiphanes of the Seleucid Empire ruled over Judea, he issued a decree that prohibited Jewish religious practices and forced worship of the Greek gods. But many refused, and some even killed the Jews who conformed. Within a year, a guerilla war broke out, and many Jews rose up to fight what turned out to be seven major battles. They ended up capturing Jerusalem and cleansing the temple of foreign gods, leading to the famous event you probably have heard about, the miraculous oil that lasted eight days when it was only enough for one, celebrated each year at Hanukkah.

These events set a precedent that lasted until the days of Jesus, who was crucified under the false charge of attempting to lead such a revolt against Rome. Eventually, these rebellions became so unruly that the Roman Empire came in and burned Jerusalem to the ground and destroyed their temple, again, in the year 70 CE. From that point forward, ritual Judaism ceased to exist, and rabbinic Judaism alone has lasted to this day, even with today's nation of Israel in power over Jerusalem some two millennia later.

Again, this doesn't have a neat parallel to today's situation with the church, as we don't hear of too many former Christians burning down churches or the like. Or do we? Many former Christians have become so angry at the church for overseeing so much harm that they actively oppose those who still have faith, confronting them at every turn. Some of these people can be ethical and fair in their approach. Many are not. That latter group causes a ruckus anytime someone even claims that they have a religious reason for doing something in the public sphere. These people go beyond protecting the freedom of religion and insist on their being freedom from religion, meaning that they want to exist in a world where Christianity's influence is reduced to such a size that it can be dragged into a bathtub and drowned. That's not just atheism. That's militancy. It comes from a place of anger and hatred, and though it purports to have religious freedom as its goal, it is no different in its approach than the Christian who bitterly complains about the war on Christmas because a courthouse isn't allowed to have a nativity scene out front.

Many of these former churchgoers simply won't let the matter rest. They have failed to grieve fully, and they get so stuck in the anger stage that they can't see past their rage. Their revolt is perhaps well-founded in that it comes from a place of legitimate outrage, but their fury often manifests itself as proselytizing and apologetics, which are exactly the sorts of things they claim to hate about Christians. These are the people who get into arguments just for their own sake and who enter debate after debate, hoping to win over minds. How is this any different from the Christians who do the same? Remember the lesson from an earlier chapter: Anger can be good in the short term, but be careful that you do not become the very thing you are angry against.

Many people who still go to church are militant revolters as well. These are the people who profess to want religious liberty for themselves, but in doing so prohibit the freedom of people with whom they disagree and over whom they have any control. Famous cases include Hobby Lobby's refusal to cover contraceptives as part of its health care provision for their employees, even though corporations do not necessarily have the right to break the law for religious reasons. That didn't protect Hobby Lobby's rights; it enforced their beliefs on their employees. Similarly, there was the well-known case of Kentucky county clerk Kim Davis, who gained national attention by refusing to sign marriage certificates for gay couples out of her belief that those marriages were sinful. As a public servant, she did not have such a right, and she was convicted of contempt of court for her defiance of the law. That by itself may have been ethical, but she also refused to allow her subordinates to sign the certificates, meaning that she was enforcing her beliefs onto people who didn't share them. That's not religious liberty; that's religious oppression. It's a revolt.

Both of these ways, therefore, present a problem. Total abandonment of your former principles and beliefs is, at best, a kind of bargaining, but more often, it's a kind of denial. It's a hope that you can simply replace what you've lost with something else, and it refuses to admit that anything's changed. The abandoners simply assimilate into the new culture, totally forgetting what led them to become the people they were in the first place. They leave behind their values, their beliefs about the world, and their former principles for the comfort of never having to think about them again. Similarly, revolt is just getting stuck in anger (or maybe a kind of rebellion against depression), and this is just as problematic for the non-churchgoer as it is for the person who still attends. It comes from a place of contempt, not compassion. It's spite, not love. Both of these options, then, simply won't do. They aren't usually wholehearted, and they don't represent what many of us wish to become. There must be another way.

Jeremiah's Third Way

Surprisingly enough, the Bible presents a third option. It comes to us in the same chapter as that famous verse you probably once had underlined or even displayed in your home: "'For I know the plans I have for you,' declares the LORD, 'plans to prosper you and not to harm you, plans to give you hope and a future'" (Jeremiah 29:11). That verse has meant so much to so many people that it's often ripped out of its context and meant to apply to anyone who reads it. It was written to and for the exiles from Jerusalem, and it now speaks to all exiles from their homeland, even the homeland of the American church.

But it doesn't exist in a vacuum. It comes surrounded by the Lord's decree for how people should live in exile. It begins with a declaration of its immediate audience: "This is what the LORD Almighty, the God of Israel, says to all those I carried into exile from Jerusalem to Babylon" (v. 4). Notice the phrasing there. Did you catch it? "To all those *I* carried into exile" (emphasis ours). It was Babylon that did the capturing, but it's God who takes the credit— and the blame. That's an important distinction because many people feel like it was the church that pushed them out, but God is not content to shift blame onto merely a set of people. He takes it for himself. So if you have a beef, it's with God. That's important because even though he did not necessarily do the shoving, he takes on the responsibility for it. You can blame the institution all you want, but it's God who ultimately bears the burden. This is why it's so difficult for many people who find themselves outside the church. They think they can carry on with their faith alone because it was the church that was the instrument of their pain. But God says that it was *he* who carried people into exile. The American church may have been like Israel, full of corruption and betrayal, and the secular culture may have been like the pagan captors of Babylon. But it's God who accepts the fault. We can't blame the church or culture without blaming God. He doesn't leave us that option.

Instead, God gives a command to the exiles about what to do: "Build houses and settle down; plant gardens and eat what they produce" (v. 5). In other words, settle into your discomfort. You may never find your way back home. You may never again be the person you once were. You may always be an exile. That's immensely painful. But God is saying to bloom where you're planted, even though where you're planted isn't a place of your choosing. You're supposed to make a home wherever you are. If it's outside the institutional church for good, plant your garden there and seek after the Lord. If it's inside the church finally, all the better. And if it's somewhere in the grey area in between, that's okay too. Just plant your garden and build your life in earnest, seeking after your sense of God with all your heart. It's perfectly fine to deconstruct your faith as long as you do so honestly and without bitterness, with self-reflection and candor and not disdain. Bloom where you're planted.

God goes on, "Marry and have sons and daughters; find wives for your sons and give your daughters in marriage, so that they too may have sons and daughters. Increase in number there; do not decrease" (v. 6). That means you should build a life and a future for yourself. You shouldn't wallow in self-pity over your spiritual estate. You should carry on with your life, even though you're in exile. Depression over your condition is not a long-term option. It's appropriate to lament for a time, but in the end, you simply are where you are. You may never return, so it's fitting to build a home there instead of living in a shack for the rest of your life. Too many people deconstruct their faith without ever trying to put it back together again. They tear apart what they used to believe but never settle on what they believe now. That's useful, but it doesn't lead to a solution. It leaves you, instead, living in a grief-shanty that will fall apart at a stiff breeze. You need a home, a well-built structure, and that means settling into your spiritual residence, wherever that may be. That means doing more than tearing your faith down. You have to build something back up to replace it, some set of core values and beliefs that define who you are and what you stand for.

That all sounds like good advice so far, but it's the next section that drives many people batty: "Also, seek the peace and prosperity of the city to which I have carried you into exile. Pray to the LORD for it, because if it prospers, you too will prosper" (v. 7). That means that we should pray for our home, even for the people who exiled and captured us. It's not okay to hold a permanent grudge against the American church, nor against the secular culture in which you find yourself exiled. Revolt is not a serious or effective option. We must not resent the people who hurt us or the people who received us from that hurt. Instead, we should seek their peace and prosperity. That requires us to pray for and seek the good of the church, even for the ones who put us through agony, that they may flourish and come to know God more. It requires us also to pray for and seek the good of our culture, even for the ones who reject God, that they may thrive and become more aware of the God who loves them.

This is the third option, the way of the holy exile, to love God and to love people, to build your own home and to build up the homes of others, and to bless the land you find yourself in. In doing this, you find your way toward repentance for your complicity in what you have done, to forgiveness for what others have done, and to acceptance of what God has done. This is the way forward, the path toward finding meaning in your exile. What does this look like practically? How do you live this out? It turns out the Bible has an answer to that too.

From Fasting to Fire

In the book of the Bible called Daniel (after whom one of the authors of this book is named), there is a series of stories about how some exiles lived out Jeremiah's third way of existing in exile. Their names were Daniel, Hananiah, Mishael, and Azariah. You probably know Daniel from the lion's den and the latter three from their Babylonian names: Shadrach, Meshach, and Abednego. It's there that we make our first point. These men accepted Babylonian names, one of which (Abednego) pays direct homage to a foreign god, Nebo, the Babylonian god of wisdom. Since Israel's fall had a lot to do with idolatry, you'd be right to ask if this is a crisis of conscience for these exiles. But it doesn't appear to be. They take on these foreign, idol-honoring names without much fuss, and they wear their clothes and serve in their government. They become civic leaders in Babylon, and they serve the same king who carried them into exile. They seek his good and the good of their oppressors, even though this is the same nation that destroyed their homeland.

This is the same way that we have to live in our church and our culture. The church may have pushed you out, but the way of the earnest exile is still to honor it and seek its good. And your surrounding culture may try to change your name by taking on roles and seeking after its good, even though it has collapsed the church in on itself. But true wholeheartedness calls us to pursue its benefit and to contribute to its well-being, even though it hurt us and still oppresses us, and even when our ethics are challenged to their core.

The prophet Daniel and his friends lived this out on the very first page of their tale. The receiving of foreign names that honored another god was not the point of their contention, but rather the eating of food sacrificed to that god. That presented a choice for the four friends. They could have abandoned their principles and given in to the new culture altogether. And they could have violently revolted, likely to their own deaths. But they don't do either. Instead, they nonviolently resist by finding a third way. Daniel asks their overlords, "Please test your servants for ten days: Give us nothing but vegetables to eat and water to drink" (Daniel 1:12) and then to "compare our appearance with that of the young men who eat the royal food, and treat your servants in accordance with what you see" (v. 13).

Now, this isn't a special diet that you should follow just because it's in the Bible (sorry, Chris Pratt). Rather, it's of special significance because it means total abstinence from something dedicated to an idol other than the true God. This was a big deal because participating in eating that food would have meant a personal acceptance of that god. This goes beyond having a name that honors it. This goes into actual worship territory.

But these men don't give in, and they don't revolt, either. Rather, they nonviolently protest, even to the point of endangering their own lives. This happens again just two chapters later when three of the men (Shadrach, Meshach, and Abednego) were in charge of an estate in the Babylonian plain of Dura. There, the king "made an image of gold, sixty cubits high and six cubits wide" (Daniel 3:1) and commanded that "whoever does not fall down and worship [it] will immediately be thrown into a blazing furnace" (v. 6).

This again presents a crisis of conscience for the Israelite men. They know they cannot worship a false god, and they will not bow down before the statue. That's idolatry, which is the very thing that got them exiled in the first place. But they also know that they can't violently revolt because that goes against God's will too. Rather, they seek that third way, a nonviolent subversion of the law. When everyone else bows down and worships, Shadrach, Meshach, and Abednego just stand there in protest, possibly with backs turned. The king calls them before him and chastises them, saying, "If you do not worship it, you will be thrown immediately into a blazing furnace. Then what god will be able to rescue you from my hand?" (v. 15).

But they don't give in. And they don't pull out any swords, either. Instead, they use their mouths to stand up to the king. "King Nebuchadnezzar, we do not need to defend ourselves before you in this matter. If we are thrown into the blazing furnace, the God we serve is able to deliver us from it, and he will deliver us from Your Majesty's hand. But even if he does not, we want you to know, Your

Majesty, that we will not serve your gods or worship the image of gold you have set up" (vv. 16–18).

They offer no serious defense, even proclaiming that they need none. There are no excuses, no clever ways out, just a declaration of their intention. Notice their faith here. They fully believe that God can save them, even though they admit that he may not. Either way, they are prepared to die for their beliefs without resistance.

How many of us can say the same? So many of us have given in so many times when we've been asked to violate our consciences. Lest you think this is other people, really think about it. No one is asking you to bow down before an idol of gold, but what about the idol of greed? Does that quarterly bonus mean more than your ethics? Or the idol of sex. Is an hour of thrill really worth sacrificing your integrity? You can call those merely earthly things if you want, but so are all idols. The two primary idols Israel got in trouble for worshipping were Baal, the god of power, and Asherah, the goddess of sex. Nothing much changes, does it? Every day, our culture asks us to bow down to these idols too, and every week, many churches bow down before the idols of political power, greed, and personal advancement. The way of the exile is to bow down to none of these but to swear allegiance instead to God, even if that means being rejected by your friends, by your employer, or by your church.

Giving in is not the right option. Nor is a mean or violent approach, either by words or actions. The ethic of the exile is to submit to the power of the authorities without giving in to their idol-worship. And that's exactly what Shadrach, Meshach, and Abednego do. They are taken by the king and thrown into a giant furnace. So hot is the fire that it kills the soldiers who drag them into it. But the lives of the three friends are miraculously spared. Instead, "the fire had not harmed their bodies, nor was a hair of their heads singed; their robes were not scorched, and there was no smell of fire on them" (v. 27). God delivered his exiles from death.

Now, God does not always do this (God does not save Stephen from being stoned to death in the book of Acts, for example), but this was done here so that the testimony of these men would live on. Even the king says that "no other god can save in this way" (v. 29), demonstrating that he now has some measure of belief in the true God. This is what our lives will do, too, if we continue to fight for our faith in God in this third way. You may have deconstructed your faith to deal with the pain of church, but we believe that putting it back together again will provide the best path for discovering who you were born to be. Like it or not, for former churchgoers, church and God are part of your identity, no matter how much you reject them as part of your present experience. They changed you, formed you, and molded you. The path forward isn't to go out and worship the false gods of greed, power, or lust. The path forward is to accept who you truly are and stand up to those false gods. Those idols have no place in a whole heart or in the soul of an exile.

Shadrach, Meshach, and Abednego had every reason to believe that God had abandoned them and the Israelite people. After all, God was the one who took responsibility for their destruction as a nation and for the exile in which they then found themselves. They had probably fought within their souls about the goodness of a God who would allow such calamity or even engineer it. And they had probably blamed their home nation of Israel for their condition. But none of that prevented them from exercising their conscience. They had deconstructed and reconstructed their faith, and in doing so, they had found themselves whole.

In the same way, you probably have every reason to doubt God's righteousness. He allowed his church to hurt you, after all, and he even takes responsibility for your leaving it and becoming an exile. But just like with these three friends, you have the opportunity to continue in your way to seek after God, even though he may not save you. You don't have to give into the idolatry of your former church or your present culture. And you don't have to angrily resist and hold onto bitterness about them. The way forward is to submit to their authority even unto spiritual death, even unto losing yourself, because in doing so, you will find yourself. As Jesus puts it, "Whoever finds their life will lose it, and whoever loses their life for my sake will find it" (Matthew 10:39).

We see this story played out again in Daniel 6, with the famous story of the lion's den when Daniel refuses to pray to the king. And we see it again in the New Testament when Jesus nonviolently submits himself to crucifixion on a Roman execution rack under false charges, feeling abandoned by a God he felt had "forsaken" him (see Mark 15:34). Just ponder that for a moment. However separated you feel from God or the church, however exiled, however evicted from his presence, it pales in comparison to the estrangement of Christ on the cross from his Father in heaven. The church rejected you, and it seems like God has too. But Jesus's followers abandoned him, his Father led him to the cross, and the very people he was there to save had him executed. Jesus was the ultimate exile, yet he chose this third way: a nonviolent protest, a prophetic subversion that cost him his life.

We are called to nothing less. Even if you don't believe that Jesus was divine, his example is one we can all learn from. He didn't fight back, nor did he give in. He didn't revolt, nor did he relinquish. He did not resist, nor did he surrender. He instead submitted himself to the natural result of his faith when it was juxtaposed against the idolatry of his people and his culture.

Even if you've abandoned following Jesus, abandoning your principles is not an option. Even if you've assimilated into your culture, taking on its gods is not an option. Even if you want to strike out and seek to destroy either the church or the culture with your words or actions, revolt is not an option. Being a blessing to your culture and the church is the way. Seeking the good of both is the way. Planting your garden where you find yourself is the way. Maintaining your conscience when you are asked to worship false gods is the way.

Don't give in, and don't give up.

Further Questions

1. If you grew up in church and left it, why? What has happened to that church and other people who went there?
2. In the past or today, have you chosen the way of abandonment or the way of revolt against your church or your culture? Or both? What has that looked like for you?
3. What do you make of God's command to "build houses and settle down; plant gardens and eat what they produce" (Jeremiah 29:5) while in exile? What does this mean for your life?
4. What have you learned from the stories of the four exiles in Babylon? How did they bless their new nation? How did they maintain their integrity?

8

Fireside Chat

A couple dozen or so people sat around a campfire in the region of Caesarea Philippi in about the year 30 CE. They told stories. They laughed. They ate what little food they had carried with them. One of them perhaps told scary tales and made shadow puppets with his hands and the firelight. All was merry.

But one of the men, their leader, spoke up. He asked, "Who do people say the Son of Man is?" (Matthew 16:13). That stopped all the enjoyment in its tracks. Suddenly, the crackling fire and crickets were all they could hear. No one wanted to answer. Each man looked at the other for a response.

"Son of Man" was a title they had heard before. It was their leader's favorite name for himself, a reference to the dreams of the prophet Daniel some six centuries earlier. They had heard about those dreams. Scary stuff. Whenever their leader used that name for himself, a shiver went down their spine. Most people didn't get it. Others were simply confused by it. A few were scared of it. Every time he employed that title, his followers were afraid that he would lose his audience.

But he didn't. Despite their concerns, it always seemed to work. There was something about this leader, this rabbi, this Jesus, that was utterly irresistible. He just couldn't be stopped. He spoke to a whole legion of men not too long before and fed them, which certainly raised an eyebrow or two from the Romans. But he had never been violent about it, and he certainly had never led a revolt. He was just a highly charismatic leader who had a knack for getting people to listen. Right?

They could tell by each other's answers that they were hedging their bets. One of them stood up and pretended to walk like a mummy. "Some say John the Baptist" (v. 14), he squawked, putting his thumb to his throat and slicing it to represent what had happened to their beloved friend. But he was joking since most of them had met John earlier. They all laughed, but then their chuckles descended into somber, funereal silence. Crickets and crackles again.

Another one of them spoke up just to break the tension. "Others say Elijah" (v. 14), he suggested. Elijah had been the great prophet before King Ahab all those centuries ago, proclaiming God's justice on an unholy nation. Jesus had taken on a similar attitude toward some unrepentant towns not too long ago, so they all agreed that Jesus could be Elijah. After all, the late prophet Malachi had predicted that Elijah would come back to "turn the hearts of the parents to their children, and the hearts of the children to their parents" (Malachi 4:6). Jesus had largely proclaimed a message of peace, so this made all sorts of sense. They all nodded and vocally agreed.

But Jesus didn't appear satisfied. He cocked an eyebrow and shook his head. He put his hand out, suggesting that he wanted to hear more. "Jeremiah," one of his followers almost shouted. "Still others, Jeremiah" (Matthew 16:14), he said, now in greater control of his voice. "Or one of the prophets" (v. 14), he hedged, unsure of his suggestion. There were no biblical prophecies of Jeremiah coming back, and Jesus didn't really sound anything like him, so the other men around the campfire just chuckled at the suggestion.

Jesus interrupted their laughter. "But what about you?" (v. 15) he dropped into the conversation. Everything went silent again. Crackles and crickets. Even the wind seemed to stop whispering in their ears. Jesus had never really asked their personal opinions before. He had declared his truth, and these were merely the people who followed. Their points of view had never been requested.

Without even discussing it, the men all looked to Simon, who merely stared into the campfire, muttering to himself some words that they could barely hear. Jesus looked him straight in the eye. "Who do you say I am?" (v. 15) Jesus asked, beckoning Simon to speak up and boring his gaze into his soul.

Simon finally raised his voice. "You are the Messiah" (v. 16), he said confidently. This notion had crossed some of his friends' minds before, but they had never really said it out loud. Jesus had not even said it of himself, and the few times others had mentioned it, he was quick to silence them. That Simon would declare this, even in private, implied a great amount of respect and imparted upon Jesus the role of Israel's savior from oppression.

But Simon wasn't done. Almost as if he hadn't finished his sentence yet, he added, "the Son of the Living God" (v. 16). This shocked the men around the campfire. They had heard people foretell that the Messiah was coming, and they had even heard it suggested that Jesus was him. But "Son of the Living God" was a transformative phrase in their thinking, one that they had all used when Jesus walked on water, but also one they scarcely believed. They had seen great miracles, but their minds had not yet wrapped themselves around the concept of what that meant. It was easy enough to say that when they saw Jesus jaunt across the sea and calm a storm with only his voice. But here, around a mere campfire, with no miracles occurring around them and in the quiet of the starry night, for Simon to speak up and say this was wholly life-changing. No man sitting there would forget this moment. It meant that Jesus wasn't just Israel's Messiah. He was Israel's God. Following him was only part of what they were called to do. If they were to believe what Simon had said, worshipping him was now mandatory. Jesus, it seemed, was leaving them no other option.

Jesus replied, "Blessed are you, Simon son of Jonah" (v. 17). That word *blessed* was one Jesus had used before, a note of special significance. He had said it of the very people he was trying to reach with his message: the poor in spirit, the mourners, the humble, the righteous, the merciful, the pure in heart, the peacemakers, and the persecuted. Everything Simon never wanted to be, but everything Jesus had called him to become. At that moment, Jesus associated Simon's faith with all the things Jesus said he valued in a person.

But Jesus doesn't stop there. "For this was not revealed to you by flesh and blood, but by my Father in heaven" (v. 17). Jesus was telling Simon that, due to his faith, he had received a special connection with the God of Israel, like the prophets of old and even like Jesus himself. He was saying that Simon had a direct link to the same Spirit of God that empowered great men and women to do great things. This was the highest possible compliment Jesus had to offer someone like Simon, one he had never said before and would never say again. Simon probably beamed with joy with a sparkle in his eyes and puffed out his chest with pride. This conveyed a gigantic sense of honor. Simon had a massive serotonin rush going. The guys all would have cheered.

"And I tell you that you are Peter" (v. 18), Jesus interrupts their ovation, carrying on his compliment. *Peter* was not Simon's given name, but Jesus here renames him because of what he has just done. *Peter* means "rock." Rocks are solid. Rocks are foundations. Rocks are what you use to build great big things like the Temple and even whole cities. *Bedrock* and *firmament* are more literal translations, actually, the very things you use to hold up a large structure. Even more cheers.

"And on this rock I will build my church" (v. 18), Jesus continues. He hadn't used that word *church* before. It didn't mean then what we think it means today. It wasn't a building or even a holy set of people. It was an assembly gathered to deliberate and discuss what Simon just said about Jesus and for openly pondering its implications. This church, or *ekklesia*, would be a gathering of contemplation, questioning, and even controversy. It wouldn't be a group of people who all believed or thought the same way. It would be a group of people who would reflect on the divinity of Jesus and the claims his followers made about him. In the Greek context, an ekklesia wasn't a group with its mind made up. It was a group that came to make up its mind.

So few American churches today leave room for any doubt about Jesus, and it's far too easy to be branded as a heretic. But do you know what the root of that word *heretic* is? It's from the Greek *hairétikos*, meaning "able to choose." If you ask us as authors, that's what we think God wants from all of us. He doesn't desire a mindless assent to a set of beliefs. Rather, he longs for us to have the license to choose him. Oblivious automatons do him no good. He wants free, totally liberated souls to desire him back. That's what *worship* means.

So Jesus wasn't establishing his church upon absolute assent. He was establishing his church on the willingness to say what others won't, on Simon's faith to reach out for more of what it means for Jesus to be who he is. It was this about which Jesus said that "the gates of Hades will not overcome it" (v. 18). Hades was their understanding of the realm of the dead. Jesus was saying that having the free spiritual capacity to pursue him and to discuss him was the very thing that would defeat death. Jesus didn't present a command. He presented a choice.

That's what so few American churches do. They don't provide a choice. Instead, they provide a wedge, a dividing line that says you're either in or you're out. They build a fence on the otherwise blurry line between church and not-church that holds out anyone who doesn't already conform to their way of thinking and practicing. But this is not what Jesus had in mind when he said "church." He believed in an ekklesia where people took care of each other, bound by their uniting love for one another and their collective confession of sin. When Jesus said "repent," he wasn't establishing a dividing line, but rather presenting an opportunity to decide. For the first time since Adam and Eve, he gave people a real choice about their sinfulness. Finally, they could freely choose righteousness through confession and pursuing more of Jesus.

But many churches don't allow room for this. Confess your sins and get branded as unrighteous. Confess your doubts and get marked as a heretic. Confess your inner turmoil and get kicked out. That's what we've largely done. Most churches have become places where it's unsafe to be transparent or vulnerable, so of course, people have found us to be hypocritical and judgmental. We haven't overcome spiritual death. We contribute to it.

We know of a man who was baptized after he confessed Jesus as his Savior. He was twelve at the time, and the church that led him to that salvation practiced baptism by sprinkling. This is where they throw water on you rather than immerse you in a pool. When this man grew up, he eventually moved and joined a new church, one that he and his family adored because of its commitment to biblical teaching and truth. When he told his story about his conversion into the faith and his sprinkling baptism, this presented a problem for that church because they only practiced baptism by full immersion. When this man applied for membership at the church, they denied his request because of this difference in practice unless he decided to get baptized by full immersion at their church.

He refused (we think rightly), declaring that it was salvation through faith that made him a Christian and not a specific method in which a particular ritual was done. It would have been the same thing if they had declared he wasn't married because the ceremony was performed outside a church. Their opinion on the matter doesn't make the status of the relationship any less valid, nor is his having marital relations after such a ceremony adultery. That would be patently ridiculous. But that's a decent comparison to what his church was saying here. Their standard for church membership was that a person be Christian, but their definition of Christian was limited to a particular practice and not faith. They were saying that this man's faith was invalid because of how water had been used in his baptism.

And it's not that they're wrong about their commitment to full immersion baptism. They're probably right, as the Greek word *baptizo* literally means "to immerse in water." But when they held their standard of correctness up as the bar for being Christian enough to join them, they ceased being an ekklesia as Jesus had in mind. The church is supposed to be a safe space to doubt, to question, to begin believing, and to spiritually bleed. It's supposed to be a safe space to grow in faith, not a place where it's dangerous to not have it all together yet. It's upon that rock that the church is built, and it's that church that will not be overcome by death.

Jesus went on. "I will give you the keys of the kingdom of heaven," he said to his followers. "Whatever you bind on earth will be bound in heaven, and whatever you loose on earth will be loosed in heaven" (v. 19). Many churches have interpreted this to mean that they have absolute authority over their congregants because salvation must, therefore, come through the church. But it doesn't. Salvation comes through faith, which we argue should be able to be worked out in church but is not exclusive to it. Jesus doesn't give his keys to the kingdom of heaven to just any church, but to the ekklesia he just described. The one that allows questions, concerns, and confessions to be heard, the one of diversity and inclusion. The assembly. Again, this isn't a group of people who already have their minds made up. It's a group of people who come to work together to make up their minds. Their minds may not all end up in the same place, and that's okay. They may all have wildly different beliefs about Jesus, and that's okay. They may all have a variety of understandings of their salvation, and that's okay. Church is supposed to be a place of involvement, not eviction.

It's precisely because Jesus creates such a church that it holds the keys to the kingdom of heaven. The church is "a great multitude that no one could count, from every nation, tribe, people and language, standing before the throne and before the Lamb. They were wearing white robes and were holding palm branches in their hands. And they cried out in a loud voice: 'Salvation belongs to our God, who sits on the throne, and to the Lamb'" (Revelation 7:9–10). If you can bring yourself to confess that Jesus saves, no matter what that looks like to you personally, you belong in the ekklesia.

But wait. There's more. Because Jesus wasn't done talking yet about what it meant to believe in him as Messiah. "From that time on Jesus began to explain to his disciples that he must go to Jerusalem and suffer many things at the hands of the elders, the chief priests and the teachers of the law, and that he must be killed and on the third day be raised to life" (Matthew 16:21). This was incomprehensible to his followers. The cheering at Simon's confession would have stopped cold. Crackles and crickets again. We're not given the exact words of Jesus's statement here, but the broad nature of the text suggests that he had to tell them this several times, almost as if they just didn't—or perhaps wouldn't—get it. We believe this because Simon "took him aside and began to rebuke him. 'Never, Lord!' he said. 'This shall never happen to you!'" (v. 22).

We suspect that Simon's rebuke was in hushed tones, where only the two of them could hear, but we also suspect that Jesus's response wasn't quiet at all: "Get behind me, Satan!" (v. 23). He probably shouted this loudly enough for the others to hear. This was a stunning reprimand. To equate Simon with Satan, the same force that tortured Job, must have stopped him in his tracks. In Greek, it's almost word for word what Jesus said to Satan when he was being tempted in the wilderness. Simon would have been completely bewildered and beside himself with grief at hearing this. His soul would have whimpered at the very thought.

And so should ours. Our American church has done the same thing as Simon. We have so focused on the divinity of Christ that we have forgotten his humanity, his mortality, and his vulnerability. He is so much more than a God. He is human. Glorified in his resurrection, yes, but still a human to this day. He's not some disembodied spirit in the clouds. He's much closer than that. He is able "to empathize with our weaknesses" (Hebrews 4:15), meaning that he had them too. He didn't sin, but he was tempted to do so. He struggled, he strived, and he persevered. He sought truth and wholeheartedness. He pursued justice and righteousness with everything he had. He has scars and wounds. He is "the image of the invisible God" (Colossians 1:15), meaning that he's more than just a deity. He's a connectable, relatable human. Jesus died. We celebrate the cross as a victory, but the notion of this was enough to make his disciples doubt that he had any idea what he was talking about. The very idea of a cross made Jesus a victim, not a victor, a tragedy and a trauma. The cross is only a win because of the resurrection, but we must sit in the agony of his death before we spring to the liberation of his life. Jesus was vulnerable.

That means we have to be too. That means the church must be a place where people can bring their wounds to be healed, a holy space where doubt and acceptance can intermingle in the beautiful marriage called faith. Peter wasn't doubting Jesus, which is acceptable. He was telling Jesus who he thought Jesus should be, which is not. Jesus has left us the options of doubt and difference, but not denial. He had the essential mission of sacrificing himself on the cross for the forgiveness of sins. American churches so often try to take Jesus off that cross by saying people must deal with their sins before they can come there. It's fine to have been an alcoholic, but you have to have given it up before you can be taken seriously. It's fine to have used pornography in the past, but you must be chaste from it before you can be accepted here. You must get sin totally off your heart under your own power before Jesus can save you. That's been our message. And Jesus says to us as a church, "Get behind me, Satan!"

Every time we reach for power, he says that. Every time we pursue privilege, he says that. Every time we put up barriers between people and the cross, he says that. Every time we deify ourselves, push people away, or seek earthly gain, he says that.

"You are a stumbling block to me" (v. 23), Jesus continues. We, like Simon, so often get in the way of the mission, presenting hurdle after hurdle for people to jump over before they can get in so we can remain safe from outside influences. God loves us so much, but we spurn that love by not carrying it forward to others. Let us be clear: If the church is not a safe space to ask honest questions and to seek after honest answers as you earnestly pursue what it means to follow Jesus, then it is not an ekklesia. It's just a club where people happen to sing songs about God. It's a stumbling block to the mission of Jesus. It stands in his way of getting the job done.

That word for "stumbling block" is the Greek *skandalon*, which means "forcing to bow." It's where we get the word *scandal* from. In this, Jesus is saying the same thing about Simon that he said about Satan in Matthew 4:9. Simon is trying to get Jesus to worship him. This isn't by bowing down before him in person or falling prostrate or singing praises to Simon. Rather, this is about conforming to Simon's way of thinking, submitting to his understanding of Jesus's role as Messiah instead of to God's.

Make no mistake: Churches do this too. So many of us are either toxic in our ranting about what we perceive as sin, or cynical in our belief that we alone have it right, or else so saccharine that it doesn't appear that we live in the real world. All of these compel the mission of Jesus to our understanding of the nature of grace. We try to make Jesus worship us instead of the other way around. We try to make Jesus conform his way of thinking into ours. We try to make Jesus renew his comprehension of mercy and atonement to fit our petty distinctions and squabbles. We try to reduce the God of heaven into a denominational or political hack. We try to hijack the cross. To that, Jesus says we are a "stumbling block" (v. 23).

Why? Because we "do not have in mind the concerns of God, but merely human concerns" (v. 23). That's a somewhat polite translation, but this is Jesus saying to Simon, and to us, that we have it wrong. We haven't got the wrong practice or even the wrong systematic theology. Rather, we've got the wrong vision of the world. We don't see it as Jesus sees it. We're so fixated on gaining sociopolitical power and shoring up our defenses so we never have to think critically again that we have left outside our churches the very souls Jesus is trying to save. We have played the harlot, lusting after the idols of power and greed, instead of retaining our commitment to loving Jesus and serving his mission "to seek and to save the lost" (Luke 19:10). We have rejected them instead of reaching out to them, just because they're different from us.

This is why Jesus's next words are so important: "Whoever wants to be my disciple must deny themselves and take up their cross and follow me. For whoever wants to save their life will lose it, but whoever loses their life for me will find it" (Matthew 16:24–25). We imagine Jesus might have taken each of Simon's arms and made a harsh hammering motion into his wrists to emphasize his point. Jesus was going to die. Simon would have to follow in that path and sacrifice himself for the sake of the mission too.

We're meant to sacrifice ourselves for the sake of others, even at their own hands. We're meant to love with everything we've got, even to our deaths. We're meant to give up on earthly things, worldly power, and human points of view. Jesus requires us to create ekklesias where it's safe to process that, where we give up on our sense of self for the sake of each other. Churches where we all dress the same, think the same, act the same, vote the same, and spend the same are not ekklesias. They're country clubs.

The general notion is that if you are smart and disciplined, if you studiously say nothing, if you avoid showing that you think the wrong thing, or indeed that you think at all, you can win at religion. And that's true. You can. It's even true that by winning at religion, you can gain the whole world. We've seen that throughout Western history. But Jesus asks, "What good will it be for someone to gain the whole world, yet forfeit their soul? Or what can anyone give in exchange for their soul?" (v. 26). We as authors think the American church has largely forfeited its soul. Not every church, not every time, but as a whole. We forfeited our soul when we cared more about saving traditional marriage than we did about the lives and souls of those trying to get married. We forfeited our soul when we raged against the abortion of unborn children, only to forget about caring for those children if they were carried to term, particularly when it comes to trafficking. We forfeited our soul when we chastised people about sex instead of showing them the way to true intimacy. And we forfeited our soul when we sold ourselves after political power. We gained so much in terms of earthly, corporeal influence, but we gave up on the heavenly, eternal power found in Jesus.

Jesus told his disciples what would happen as a result of that: "The Son of Man is going to come in his Father's glory with his angels, and then he will reward each person according to what they have done" (v. 27). Which side of that do you want to be on? Which side do you want your church to be on? We're not talking about eternal salvation here, or heaven and hell. We're talking about eternal reward. We don't gain points by being exclusive. Nor do we gain points by purifying our congregations of heretics and nonbelievers. We gain points by including others, by reaching across the line, and by tearing down the fence. We gain points by removing all roadblocks on the way to Jesus and by talking about him—not our beliefs about him, but *him*—with everyone we meet. We gain points by serving, by submitting, and by sacrificing. We gain points by loving.

So we have to give up on the notion that our churches need to be purer. No, they need to be messes, full of contradictions and disagreements. They need to be full of imperfect people living imperfect lives with imperfect beliefs. There is no room for self-righteousness. No room for self-importance. No room for self-worship. There is room, however, for all people who try to pursue Jesus, whatever that means to them, chasing after God with all their heart, soul, mind, and strength. It's only when we do that that we truly join Christ's mission, take on Christ's cross, and become Christ's ekklesia.

Further Questions

1. Read Matthew 16:13–27 on your own. What do you make of this passage? What does it mean for Jesus to be "the Son of the Living God" (v. 16)?

2. What has been your experience of the American church? Has it been an open and diverse space? What has been your reaction to it?

3. How have you been a "stumbling block" (v. 23) to the mission of Jesus? How has your church been one?

4. If you have any influence in a church community, what can you do to make your church more of an ekklesia like Jesus envisions?

9

Is the Church Really the Best God Can Do?

So we're left with a conundrum. The American church is broken, at least in large part. Sure, there are some truly amazing churches out there. We've been to several. And even in otherwise problematic ones, there are loads of good, Jesus-loving, people-caring Christians. But after all our experience in the American church spanning a combined eight decades, we have to admit that such churches are rare. At this point, you may wonder what a "good" church looks like and how to find one. We have some advice on that later, but first, we must take a more thorough look at one particular question that nags this discussion. Namely, this: Is the church the best that God can do?

After all, churches are full of imperfect people imperfectly finding their way. The American church seems to have institutionalized hypocrisy and lifted it up to some form of high art. Churches are often messy, exclusive, self-contradictory, and even duplicitous. One such area comes from the church's response to the LGBTQ movement. We know of one person who came out as gay sometime before she attended a church. She had been flatly rejected by several churches when she opened up about her sexuality, but she kept trying. All the while, she struggled with what it meant to follow Jesus and stay true to herself at the same time. It was a constant battle inside her soul. During this time, she remained abstinent, believing that God called sex to be explored inside of marriage, and she didn't even date, thinking she should figure out what she could about Jesus before she reached out romantically. In all ways, she submitted to Christ.

Eventually, she decided to start serving at her church. She was particularly interested in leading children in musical worship. The church she attended had a wonderful kids ministry, and she wanted to be a part of it. So she signed up. She knew other people who had done the same who got responses back within hours, but she didn't hear back for weeks. It was over a month. We were not privy to the exact response from the church, but the gist of it was that they did not believe that a person living a sinful life could be trusted to lead children in worshipping Jesus and that they would not commend to her care the souls of young ones whom she might confuse.

Just imagine that. You've sacrificed your sense of sexuality by remaining chaste and not even dating while you try to sort out what you believe about Jesus, but just because you've been open about that, you're denied any position of leadership. Even though you're not actively sinning. The problem wasn't with her choices, as she wasn't actively participating in any form of sexuality or courtship. The problem was with her identity. Just the fact that she was attracted to women. Being open about being gay simply wasn't an option. She still attends that church faithfully, and she's taken on the role of filling communion cups with wafers and juice, which we guess is the church's way of saying it's okay for her to participate in preparing a holy sacrament but not okay for her to ever, ever open her mouth about herself. She can be trusted with the body and blood of Jesus, but not his children.

Is that the best God has to offer us, a broken, messed-up system with broken, messed-up values, made up of broken, messed-up people?

Actually, yes. It is.

You see, you're imperfect. Shocker, right? You may not have found your way to believing in a God of the universe who has moral standards, but you have to admit, if only to yourself, that you have failed to live up to even your own standards, much less his. Even if you're reaching out for righteousness with everything you have, you're still missing the mark. You lie. You cheat. You objectify. You envy. You fall short. You dishonor others and yourself. You may not believe in God's laws, but you know you've violated your own. You're what the Bible calls a "sinner."

But you're also the person you've forgiven the most. Even those of us who find ourselves lost in spirals of shame have smeared over most of our sinful pasts and patterns. You lie to your boss about something you failed to follow up on, but you're not as bad as such-and-such, so you're fine. You undress a person with your eyes every time you see them, but you're okay because you would never act on it. You say yes ma'am and no ma'am to your mother, but you make fun of her and mar her name to your friends behind her back. Your internet search history is riddled with lapses in judgment, but it's okay because you're "not an addict." In all these ways, you've consistently given yourself a pass.

Now imagine a whole group of people doing that all the time. Imagine a gathering of people who are constantly giving themselves passes but never doing the hard work of changing their negative behavioral patterns. Imagine a congregation full of people who have grace on themselves, but not on others. That's what most churches look like. They haven't gone through the tough trudging of digging out the diseased vines inside their souls.

Churches are broken because people are broken. And that's something God can easily work with—if they are open about that. And that's a big if. Most churches don't do this. Most churches have institutionalized hypocrisy and covering up. But the truly good churches out there, the ekklesias, have put their scars and even their open wounds on display for all to see. They're the ones we should all seek to be like. They're the ones who are following Jesus.

By this point, it should come as no surprise to you that the Bible gives an example of this. It happens when the apostle Paul enters the city of Ephesus in the book of Acts. Take a look.

> Paul entered the synagogue and spoke boldly there for three months, arguing persuasively about the kingdom of God. But some of them became obstinate; they refused to believe and publicly maligned the Way. So Paul left them. He took the disciples with him and had discussions daily in the lecture hall of Tyrannus. This went on for two years, so that all the Jews and Greeks who lived in the province of Asia heard the word of the Lord. (Acts 19:8–10).

That starts innocently enough. Paul is spreading the word about Jesus. This is what all churches should be doing, and most are. The reason for the lack of faith in America has virtually nothing to do with people not hearing about it. Almost everyone in the United States has at least heard of Jesus, and most acknowledge some of the claims about him. What Paul did in Ephesus has been done in America. Congratulations. But there's more.

> God did extraordinary miracles through Paul, so that even handkerchiefs and aprons that had touched him were taken to the sick, and their illnesses were cured and the evil spirits left them. (vv. 11–12)

Now we're onto something the church doesn't usually do in the United States. Nearly all churches recognize the miracles of the Bible, but few are left who believe in active miracles today. We're not here to make an argument for whether or not such miracles could or would take place today. That's a debate for systematic theologians. It's not the miracles here that interest us. It's their result. Keep reading.

> Some Jews who went around driving out evil spirits tried to invoke the name of the Lord Jesus over those who were demon-possessed. They would say, "In the name of the Jesus whom Paul preaches, I command you to come out." Seven sons of Sceva, a Jewish chief priest, were doing this. One day the evil spirit answered them, "Jesus I know, and Paul I know about, but who are you?" Then the man who had the evil spirit jumped on them and overpowered them all. He gave them such a beating that they ran out of the house naked and bleeding. (vv. 13–16)

This, we believe, is the same error that many churches make today. Put the miraculous nature of the story aside if you can. Try not to think about demon possession. It's weird. We get that. Instead, try to think about this as a metaphor for what the church has done in the United States. We do things in the name of Jesus and the Bible, but we do so almost entirely without power. We preach and we preach about God, but we're not making many new converts. We cry out about injustice, but very little changes. We proclaim the name of Jesus to anyone and everyone, but almost no one is listening, usually not even ourselves. We tried to drive out the demon of sin in this country through social pressure, political power, and even legislation, but that demon has come out and is now giving us a beating. It would whimper at the name of Jesus, and it might bleat at the Bible, but it doesn't recognize our power at all and has left us naked and bleeding. We have been exposed as frauds who claim the name of Jesus, but upon whom no power has come to rest.

The story goes on.

> When this became known to the Jews and Greeks living in Ephesus, they were all seized with fear, and the name of the Lord Jesus was held in high honor. (v. 17)

Notice that. It wasn't the Jews trying to drive out the demons that got people's attention fixed on Jesus. It was instead the demon's confession that it recognized Jesus and Paul. This represents the opportunity for American churches today. It was the testimony of the demon while it beat up the frauds that got people to honor God. In the same way, churches today can point to their failures and fraud, and declare their need for the power of Jesus. By giving in to the demon's power (not by sinning but by admitting that we are sinful to begin with), we proclaim the goodness of God through the confession of our sin. We've been pointing to society's sins forever, and we've always had a beef with our secular culture, but we've done very little to turn that finger back on ourselves. One wonders what would happen if churches just realized that they need Jesus too. What would happen if we confessed?

Well, the story tells us.

> Many of those who believed now came and openly confessed what they had done. A number who had practiced sorcery brought their scrolls together and burned them publicly. When they calculated the value of the scrolls, the total came to fifty thousand drachmas. (vv. 18–19)

Fifty thousand drachmas doesn't tell us much, but a drachma is about a day's wages. Assuming today's minimum wage in the United

States ($7.25 per hour) at eight hours per day times fifty thousand days, we reach a total of $2.9 million. That was the level of their confession. They were willing to burn down their economy for the sake of repentance. What would happen if American churches did the same? What if we publicly burned our unrighteousness, our greed, and our arrogance? What if we fell on the sword of our sins and accepted the consequences?

> In this way the word of the Lord spread widely and
> grew in power. (v. 20)

That's what would happen. The word of the Lord would spread widely and grow in power. Confession is the true currency of the Jesus economy. It's not about how many people are in our pews, how many dollars are in our bank account, or how many bills we've gotten passed in the local legislature. It's about repentance from our wicked ways. It's about contrition, penitence, and grievous sorrow for the wrong we have done. We have hurt people. We have starved people. We have deprived people of the grace of Jesus. We have sinned greatly. And it's time for us to openly confess what we have done. Not just to ourselves privately in some back room. Openly. We have to burn down our earthly economy of power for the true economy of confession.

It seems all too easy to confess your sins to Christ as this amorphous, invisible force, but being a Christian is so much more than mental assent to a set of beliefs, or even prayer to a largely imperceptible entity. Don't get us wrong. It's wonderful to be able to pray directly to God. That's what the indwelling of the Holy Spirit is all about. That intimacy is extraordinary. But the problem arises when we only confess to God. That allows us to hide, to mask, and to obfuscate. It allows us to cover ourselves in what appears like holiness because we have prayed away our sins, but without any person to hold us accountable, we tend to slip back into them all too easily.

This is why James admonishes us to "confess your sins to each other and pray for each other so that you may be healed" (James 5:16). "So that you may be healed," he says, meaning that you can pray all you want, but if you want true healing from sin, true release from it, you need to confess it to someone else. This doesn't mean that prayers toward God are ineffective for salvation or divine forgiveness. This does mean, however, that prayers are usually not enough for us to make substantive life change. It's just too easy to keep our sins to ourselves that way. The more wholehearted approach is to find one or two very close friends and be open about your brokenness. They don't have to be perfect people, but they shouldn't be just anybody. They should be close, loving, compassionate people who will listen to your sins privately and safely, without judgment or threat of gossip, and who will point you toward the kind of person you truly want to be and, if you're willing, toward Jesus.

Whether or not you claim Jesus anymore, confession is good for the soul. Too many people leave church thinking they are done with this for good because of the negative impacts of confessing in the wrong environment or to the wrong people. But finding those few people to confess to and then letting your guard down to reveal your true, real, messy self is absolutely essential to the wholehearted life. If you want to be a better person, if you want to grow, you must confess. Not because the Bible says so necessarily but because it's just good practice for maturity. As it turns out, the Bible has a lot of good things to say about how to live life, even if you don't agree with it or believe in it.

The reason we believe that is because the Bible is annoyingly good at airing its characters' dirty laundry. Sure, there's the perfect Christ, but nearly every other character is a broken, messed-up person in one way or another. We're not talking about little sins, either. Abraham oppresses a slave girl and her son (who also happens to be his son). Isaac lies about his wife and submits her to possible rape just to save his skin. Jacob lies, cheats, and steals from his family. Moses murders an Egyptian. Aaron builds the golden calf and introduces idolatry to his people. King David commits adultery and engages in a murderous conspiracy. Solomon sleeps with almost everybody he can get his hands on. Peter denies Christ and is later a hypocrite about ethnic conflicts. James and John are blatantly arrogant. Paul murders Christians. And so on. The Bible is replete with examples of its heroes messing up. The Bible confesses its people's sins.

Whether you believe the Bible to be factual or not doesn't concern us. That, we realize, is a tough pill to swallow. But what it does do is compellingly present an argument for confession, not just to God but to each other. For us to know most of the sins we discussed above, most of which were private at the time, those characters would have had to tell somebody else. These stories didn't drop out of heaven on golden tablets. They were mostly told by the original characters to other people, who told them to other people, who told them to other people, who eventually wrote them down for future generations to see. Perhaps the characters didn't know that we would today be able to read about their massive personal failures, but most of them started by just telling somebody.

That's what we have to do too. Your sins may not be on display for the world to read about someday, but perhaps they need to be on display for your closest friends to know. Just imagine what would happen if you told three safe people about your struggles. You confess to them every time you mess up and aren't wholly the person you want to be. This doesn't let you wallow in shame. It lets your soul breathe free air. Yes, you'll sometimes appear like a fool in front of these people, but that's okay. Sometimes you are a fool. Now you're just being open about it so you can learn from it and grow from it. Better to look like a fool for a little while than to be one permanently because you refused to let other people help you become wiser. Wouldn't that help you become the kind of person you want to be? Wouldn't it be nice to just let it all out from time to time rather than feeling the constant need to cover up?

In the Bible, this concept is known as nakedness. In the Garden of Eden, Adam and Eve had such an intimate relationship that they "were both naked, and they felt no shame" (Genesis 2:25). Granted, this is a spousal relationship, but let's go with it. When you first meet a potential romantic partner, you are usually wary of being naked in front of them. You worry you might not look good enough. You worry they'll reject you or laugh at you. You do extra sit-ups. You put back the ice cream. You would certainly never let them see you in the bathroom. But contrast that with a long-standing marriage of fifty years. You have grown so comfortable with each other's bodies that you willingly let them see you naked, even though you're not as young and attractive as you were when you first met. You are vulnerable with your body, allowing them to care for you when you're sick and even help you do things you were once too proud to ask help for. You used to be covered and shame-filled. Now, you are naked and without shame.

And that's just with clothing. You would never reveal your bad habits and sinful patterns with someone on a first date. That's a level of vulnerability no relationship is ready for that early on. But after fifty years of trust, ups and downs, and practiced openness, you are an emotionally open book in front of that person. They know your deepest, darkest moments. They know what you are really like when the cards are on the table. They know your good and your bad—and they love you anyway. Don't you want that kind of intimacy in a relationship? Don't you long for that level of trust? Don't you want to be naked and yet without shame?

Now, we don't recommend that you rush that, romantically or otherwise, but try to fathom a group of people who are spiritually naked with each other. They reveal their flaws. They open up about their failures. They talk about their doubts and misgivings. They discuss their brokenness. Hypocrisy has no room to grow because people are too busy being real. Faking it has no place because people call each other to more. Growth happens because grit happens.

When people do the hard work of confessing their sins, they overcome those habits.

That's what church can be. That's an ekklesia.

So yes, the church is the best God has to offer when it looks like this. When it burns down the spiritual economy and confesses to each other. When it takes risks with people. When it's vulnerable and open. When it's wholehearted, that's when church happens. Many are fond of saying that the church isn't the building but the people. That's not entirely true. The church isn't really made up of people, either. It's made up of the connective tissues and tendons uniting those people. Those don't grow overnight, and they don't grow by accident. They grow by intentional exercise.

This is why attendance at church gatherings and small group activities is so important. It's not just so you can go and independently worship and "get your Jesus on," as so many are fond of doing. That's still nominal Christianity. Going to church by itself is not wholehearted. The real church, the ekklesia, is doing the hard work of overcoming your bad habits through the continual exercises of confession and vulnerability.

If you don't believe us, just ask the great people of Alcoholics Anonymous. That's not a church in the traditional sense, but we argue that it's an ekklesia because those meetings practice being naked without shame. They provide an open and safe space for people to talk about what they've done and how they're getting through their days. They are there for each other when they fall down, no matter how many times, and they establish firm relationships for helping each other learn how to live the best lives possible, even with a devastating addiction hanging around their neck. You may disagree with the religious overtones of the Twelve Steps, and you may think the process is silly, but what you can't ignore is how many of these people go on to live amazingly wholehearted lives.

That's what church can be too. It can be a safe, transformative space to be yourself and yet reach for something more. A place where it's okay to be where you are, but where you can grow into more of who you were born to be. All because the people there confess their sins, which "[purifies] us from all unrighteousness" (1 John 1:9). That isn't to say that you'll never mess up again, but it is to say that you'll continue to develop a resiliency toward those mess-ups so that you can become more of the person you want to be.

Confession is good, and it is what the church is called to be a place for. Hypocrisy dies in the light, and sin withers in the sun. But confession and vulnerability lead to love. This is the love the church in Ephesus had at first, but they didn't keep it forever. They instead let themselves fester in pretense and became frauds. Just look at what Jesus tells them:

> I hold this against you: You have forsaken the love you had at first. Consider how far you have fallen! Repent and do the things you did at first. (Revelation 2:4–5)

Many pastors talk about this passage as if the love they lost had something to do with their passion for Jesus. It might. But we argue that it was also their lack of love for each other that caused their fall. What causes a loss of love more than any other thing is a failure to be vulnerable with each other. We believe that's exactly what happened to the church at Ephesus. They had "forsaken the love [they] had at first" (v. 4), not because they had abandoned Jesus necessarily, but because they had abandoned the notion of confessing to him and each other.

So maybe this is what happened at your church. We don't know. But what we do know is that confession leads to change. If you want to grow, to transform into the fullest version of yourself, you must become vulnerable enough to share your shortcomings with others. That doesn't have to be Christians necessarily, but it must be someone. And the same thing needs to happen to churches. They need to remember what love looks like. To paraphrase Paul, it longs for relationship, but it is patient. It is challenging, but it is kind. It listens to people without envy or boasting. It is strong, but not proud. It pays attention to sin but does not dishonor others. It helps people grow, but it is not self-seeking. It hears wrongs but keeps no record of them. It does not indulge in evil but encourages wholeheartedness. It has no tolerance for deceit but rejoices in honesty. "It always protects, always trusts, always hopes, always perseveres. Love never fails" (1 Corinthians 13:7–8).

Love is everything. But just like with a good marriage, love doesn't happen by accident. It's not automatic. It's a daily choice to submit to each other, a continuous decision to be honest and to confess, an enduring vote for vulnerability. Good marriages aren't built on the first kiss. They're built on every act of wholeheartedness. In the same way, good churches are constructed on confession. It's the foundation for love, and it is indispensable. In this way, the church can be—and is—the best God has to offer.

Further Questions

1. Get out a journal. Write on a page everything you need to get off your chest. Maybe it's an area where you need to grow. Maybe it's a dark habit that's occupying your soul. Whatever it is, put this book down and do nothing else until you've got it on paper.

2. Now, write down the names of two people you can share this with. If you're married, we advise you to make one of them your spouse. Arrange a private meeting or phone call to talk about this. Practice what you will say, but don't hold anything back. You won't grow if you won't show.

3. Next, ask them to help hold you accountable for your choices and your growth. Make a regular appointment (monthly or so) to talk about it. It doesn't have to occupy your relationship, but it does need to be a part of it.

4. Finally, if you can go this far, consider praying your confession to God. If prayer isn't your thing, try meditating on the kind of person you want to be and how you can eliminate the harmful patterns you have built in your life.

10

The Revival

S ome of you may be uncomfortable with what we've said so far, particularly any people who still go to church. We've compared the American church to ancient Israel and blamed its fall on idolatry. We've said that it's powerless because its faith isn't real. We've called it a harlot. We've even likened it to Satan in the way that Jesus did about Simon Peter. And we said it needed to repent and confess. We get that this creates a tension for many readers, which is why this is the next chapter. Originally, this was later in the book, but as we read through, we realized that we have to address solutions to the problem before continuing to move forward with the symptoms of our collective sickness.

Let us at least say this: We still believe that the church is the hope of the world because we believe that faith in the good news about Jesus spread by that church is the only thing that can save us from our sin. We thoroughly affirm that the church is the Bride of Christ as a whole, meaning the church in general in the whole world. But in this book, we're not talking about the church as a whole. We're talking about the American church as represented by evangelicals, mainline Christians, liturgical Christians, Catholics, and so on, here in the United States. These organizations have collectively done so much harm to people throughout the last century of American history that we are jointly guilty of the kinds of idolatry and oppression we've mentioned so far. There are many thousands of wonderful Christians in the United States. But we're talking about the institution as it exists here. Whether it's the constant scandal plaguing the Catholic church in terms of sexual abuse, or the waffling back and forth by the mainline Christians over any given issue, or the overtly passionate pursuit of political power by the evangelicals, the American church is rife with disease.

But it doesn't have to be this way.

Do you remember revival meetings? These were the big religious events that sought the attention of the Silent Generation, the Baby Boomers, and Generation X (and some older Millennials). They littered the 1950s through the 1980s with great spiritual rallies that lasted several summer nights in a row, usually under tents, where some fiery speaker would stand up and inspire people to invite others to join so they could "come down the aisle" to receive Christ. The most famous of these preachers was Billy Graham, who led such an event for almost half a year in New York City in 1957, popularizing the movement and giving it a great amount of cultural momentum. These events were proving grounds for pastors like Oral Roberts, and they also oversaw the salvations of hundreds of thousands of Americans, if not more. (That prolonged Billy Graham event in New York City had over 2 million attendees, for example). Make no mistake: The church in the United States would look a lot more like that of Europe if it weren't for those revivals. They brought three whole generations into following Jesus. Without them, the American church would probably be effectively dead, even in the South.

Revivals provided moments of spiritual awakening for people. They forced people to open up about their flaws and to realize that they couldn't deal with them on their own. They compelled people to recognize their need for a Savior, and they urged them to do something about it. Sure, there were some manipulative elements, like fire-and-brimstone preaching, in-or-out paradigms, end-times nonsense, and the introduction of that half-truth phrase, "personal relationship with Jesus Christ." But for the most part, revivals brought about exactly what their name suggested: new life. They breathed fresh oxygen into the lungs of a dying faith, and we have a lot to thank them for. Without the great revival of 1957 and Billy Graham's resulting fame, he would not have had the social influence to integrate the otherwise racially segregated crowds at his later revivals in the South, somewhat softening the ground for the end of Jim Crow. Without revivals, a whole generation of excellent preachers and church leaders would simply not have existed, like Andy Stanley, Louie Giglio, and Craig Groeschel. They likely never would have even been Christians, much less pastors (although we suspect all three would have gone on to become excellent business leaders). And without revivals, what few churches there would be left would have been marked by their collective passivity instead of a vigorous clinging to the truth, the last vestige of a dead religion.

The spiritual crisis that revivals brought to people now needs to be brought to the church itself. In the way that revivals compelled people to repent and turn themselves toward Jesus, many churches need to do the same. We should note here that not all individual churches need to go through this process, but the American church in general should lament its complicity in the immense oppression of souls it served to engineer. We imprisoned people in the cage of religiosity when we were called to set people free from bondage. We served to encourage racism, homophobia, Islamophobia, sexism, and greed, all in the name of religious purity for the sake of political power. Our faith in the ability of people to change once they realized they needed a Savior slowly soured into a judgmental poison whenever people didn't live up to our self-righteous standards. We became more about what we were against instead of what we were for, and we gave in to the idolatry of power over and over again.

We need to repent. We need to come back to Jesus. We need a revival. Not only to reach more people for Christ, but to reach toward Christ for ourselves. We're the ones who need to come back, to realize our wrongdoing, and to make new changes in how we live. But what does this look like? How would we even start?

Element #1: Accepting the Invitation

The first thing you had to do to attend a revival was to accept an invitation to one. That sounds simple enough, but it's not. It involves making a plan, probably getting a babysitter, sacrificing a night to yourself, dressing up, driving however long, parking in a crowded lot, walking across a field, and often enduring the hot summer's night outside in the swelter and mosquitoes. All this for some music and to hear somebody talk. That's not an easy sell. What's more, what they ask you to do at a revival is kind of a lot. Stand up, sit down, sing, listen, sing some more, and then that dreaded worst one—walk down the aisle. All of this was expected, anticipated with some solemn dread and horrid waiting in the heat and the heart.

There was no avoiding it. An invitation meant you were in for something big. Just going meant you were admitting there was something your life needed. Sure, maybe you're only pacifying the friend who wouldn't stop talking about it. But what's more likely is that you know deep down that something has to change. You've built up so much anxiety, so much doubt, so much gunk. Something's got to give. So when a friend drops an invitation in your hand, on the surface, you say you'll just check it out. But underneath, you're somewhat grateful for the opportunity because it means you will finally have no excuse for not changing. You're not sure about Jesus necessarily, but you are sure that you need a change—any change.

American churches, we believe, are at this moment. We are inviting them to a revival, a major event that could change the course of their lives forever. It won't be easy. It will be uncomfortably hot, loud, and awkward. It will require them perhaps to shut down some of their operations for a while to focus on what matters. It will compel them to admit that something is, in fact, wrong, that something about them has to change, and that something about their way of doing things is broken. It will force them to confess, even if only on the inside, even if only a little, that they're not right in the head or heart. It will take a sweltering and sweaty summer night, maybe several, to come to terms with all this.

That's what a revival is, after all. It's an interruption of what's normal to focus on what's important. It's a break from the ordinary in an attempt to find the extraordinary. American churches need such an interruption. Many of our churches are broken messes of bodies, scarcely ekklesias at all. They see little growth, little organic change, little life transformation, and almost no repentance of sin because there's almost no room for confession. The good news about Jesus has become a snooze-fest, routinized to the point of soul-numbing boredom. The metamorphosis we're all called to isn't on the back burner, not because it's important to us and in the center of our attention, but because it's not even on the stove anymore. We think we're done. We think a singular salvation moment was enough, one prayer was sufficient for all our spiritual needs.

We're dead wrong. Nothing could be further from the truth.

As Paul says to the church in Corinth, "The message of the cross is foolishness to those who are perishing, but to us who *are being saved* it is the power of God" (1 Corinthians 1:18, emphasis ours). Notice what we italicized there: *are being saved*. In grammatical terms, that's the present progressive tense. It indicates something that is currently happening, not something that has already been completed. That means it's a process, not a point. That distinction requires us to commit to the idea that we may not ever be done being saved while on this earth. That's not to say that our eternity is in jeopardy, but it is to say that our present might be. We have to continue to accept the invitation to the revival, not because we need a new salvation by Christ, but because we need a continual renewal of what it means to follow him.

Christians talk a lot about being "dead in your transgressions and sins" (Ephesians 2:1), by which we often mean that a person without Jesus is spiritually dead and only becomes alive when they "come to know Christ." There's an extent to which that's biblically expressed, though that may be a difficult pill to swallow for many. But forget that chasm for a moment. Because don't many American churches seem effectively dead as well? Don't they need something new, something fresh, and some life breathed into their lungs? Aren't they, like so many of us, choking on their hypocrisy and sinfulness? Don't they, in short, need a revival?

It's time for churches to accept the invitation, to admit that something is wrong, and to finally—*finally*—do something about it. We need to show up to the revival.

Element #2: A Gospel Crisis

But what happens there? Most revivals start with some music and some Bible reading or prayer, so maybe start there. Pay attention to the words you're singing and the reading you're doing. Give heed to the little things, like the implications of calling God a Father or singing about how amazing his grace is. Don't let the ritual or the repetition pass you by. You may have heard it all before, but let it wash over you anew. Try to think of yourself as a brand-new person experiencing this for the first time. Let the appalling strangeness of it all transform you and ready your heart for the kind of change you know needs to be made. Let not one more Sunday go by without accepting the invitation to pay attention to your ways. Don't just sing the lyrics. Don't just read the Bible passages. Don't just mentally check out when people pray. Pay attention. Absorb the moment. Live in the uncertainty.

But as much as all of that is important, we all know that when it comes to a revival, it's the sermon that steals the show. Sure, people come down the aisle to "Just as I Am," but they do so because of what they just heard someone speak.

And what they just heard will surprise you. For a revival to be at its best, it needs to present a crisis for people. Truth be told, most people are already there, or else they wouldn't have come. But the sermon forces the issue. It's the difference between saying something needs to change and identifying what that something is. Most people in the audience are just self-aware enough to realize that Jesus is what's going to be presented here, but the sermon is the compelling factor because it draws a line and says there is a right way of living and a wrong way of living. It creates a crisis for people, a crisis they may not even know they need.

That shouldn't surprise you, and no, it's not necessarily manipulative. All relationships and major life decisions occur in a crisis of one form or another. By crisis, we don't mean a dangerous point. We mean a conscious choice that has consequences beyond the moment in which it takes place. This is the case in any other relationship. You either go on that third date or stay home. You either say, "I do," or you move on. You either stick it out in counseling or sign the divorce papers. Relationships are often defined by crisis points. You're not in any less of a relationship for having reached one. Crisis points are good. They force you to choose what and who you want instead of living in the same rut you've always been in. They compel you and the relationship to mature.

There is no reason why that shouldn't be true of a relationship with Jesus. Just because you're at a precipice doesn't make you any less saved. In the same way, just because a church needs a crisis doesn't make it any less of a church. We argue that it makes it more of a church because it's facing its crisis head-on instead of just going back to business as usual. It is all too easy to just do the same thing each Sunday morning, without actually paying attention to the needs of the church as a whole. We often think our homilies and hymns are enough to honor Jesus with our lives. But just as we wouldn't accept that mere church attendance on Sunday mornings is enough for a person to have a meaningful relationship with Jesus, churches who get stuck in the rut of the Sunday morning routine may have to come to a spiritual crisis to grow.

Sometimes, that crisis is forced upon a church with a sudden disruption. These are the massive existential flexes that wreak havoc on a church for a long while, like the death or retirement of a long-beloved pastor, the resignation of a disgraced church leader, a bankruptcy, or even a global pandemic like the one occurring as we write this (COVID-19). This is just like the sudden trauma in our life that causes us to grieve, and likewise, churches may have to go through some sort of grieving process like the one we described in chapter 1. These moments define a church as much as they define a person, and we should not let them go by without doing the hard work of thoroughly addressing the issue at hand. If it were a death in someone's life, we would insist that they work through it with the guidance of God, and that is exactly what we are asking churches to do when they face a natural crisis.

But in the case of a revival, a natural crisis isn't what we're talking about. The crisis presented at a revival isn't natural at all; it's manufactured. For many people, this is partly due to the emotional high that exists at such an event. We remember these times well, as they are some of the most important memories in many people's spiritual lives. These were the camps, the revival meetings, the come-to-Jesus moments, and the Easter services. These special moments charged us up the slope toward a spiritual mountaintop, and they are quite memorable for most people who attend them. Even people who leave the church often look back on these times as important. Just because the experience was manufactured doesn't make it any less real.

A wedding, for example, is a largely manufactured event. The outcome is obvious from the outset, and the decision has been made in advance. In many cases, the wedding certificate is even signed before the vows are exchanged. The event is largely for show. But that doesn't make it any less poignant or meaningful. It's still a marked event that you remember each year with anniversaries and forever with pictures. The same thing is true of graduation ceremonies. They are highly predictable and entirely for show. They could just mail you the diploma, but instead, they insist on reading your name as you cross a stage in a manufactured moment that marks your life forever.

The manufactured crisis of a revival is no different. It's planned and coordinated, but that doesn't mean it's fake. It's just done on purpose. That's because the crisis to which you are called at a revival is an important one that often doesn't happen by accident. For the presenters, many of them consider it the most important crisis you'll ever go through, but they have to get you there. They have to compel you to see that it's as vital as they say it is. That doesn't happen unintentionally. They plan, they prepare, they practice, all so you can come to that one moment where you can honestly decide about Jesus, where you can choose God or not, where you can elect eternity with him or without him.

That's the Gospel crisis, and it's the same crisis that American churches need to go through today. They need to come to a precipice and decide whether or not God is right for them. If he's not, we understand. There's nothing wrong with having a members-only club that talks about life. That's the Moose Lodge, after all. If you want that community, go get it. It's out there. But if we want to be a church, an ekklesia, then we've got to come to a crisis moment about the Gospel. It's either the most important part of what we gather for, or it's not. It's either the transformative power that can resurrect souls, or it's not. It's either the single most crucial decision a person can make, or it's not. Churches can be a messy place with a messy middle, but it all has to center around the journey of discovering Christ crucified. Anything else isn't a church at all, no matter what it calls itself.

We believe that churches must come to this moment now. We're at the last gasp before we drown, and Jesus is the only swimmer out to rescue us. No one else is coming. No one else can come. And we can't swim to save ourselves. No amount of riches or rituals can do it for us. Only Christ can save.

Element #3: Radical Transformation

We have to live like this is true, and that means things have to change. At a revival, if you come down the aisle to receive Jesus, they would typically ask you some questions. Those questions are often some combination of the following three:

1. Do you admit that you are a sinner in need of a Savior?
2. Do you believe that Jesus is your Savior and Lord?
3. Do you commit to following Jesus for all of your days?

Those questions by no means represent easy choices. Granted, each one is a simple yes or no response, and you wouldn't be going down the aisle if you weren't ready to answer yes to each one. But those are all major concessions. Confessing to being a sinner takes hard internal work. It means admitting to yourself, God, and now some pastor you barely know that you're messed up and are in dire need of something to rescue you. Let's take those questions one by one, and apply them to churches.

First, Do you admit that you are a sinner in need of a Savior? This is a bitter tonic for most people, and it therefore shouldn't surprise us that churches aren't any different. Churches are made up of people, after all, and the last thing people want to deal with is their errancy. It's all too easy to get comfortable in your sinful patterns, and this is no less true for churchgoers than for anyone else. If anything, being in a typical church makes it easier to ignore sin because everyone is socially expected to live (or at least to present) holy and perfect lives. We all wear suits, literally or figuratively, so that we don't notice each other's scars and so that others won't see ours. We see the person beside us lifting their hands in praise, never knowing that they battle with addiction and can barely get through the words about grace without choking up. We sit next to someone else who lies every time they open their mouth, but their smile and handshake are warm. Neither of these people opens up about their brokenness, even though they need to, because doing so would risk their cozy social arrangement. The church is a great place to hide your ill deeds because almost no one asks about them there. Confess once that you need Jesus (usually as a child), get dunked, and you're good for life, never having to deal with your issues.

Now, that's just at the individual level. At the corporate level, churches are traditionally horrid at confessing their fault. When there's a scandal, they tend to fire the person and move on, not addressing the underlying conditions that led to the infractions. When there's a wayward member, they tend to encourage that member to see their way out the door instead of lifting them in prayer and helping them to scour out the sin. Most churches will do anything rather than disrupt their perfect image.

We know of one church that a long while ago had a prominent deacon, the chairman in fact, who was having an open affair with a married woman at the church. In many circumstances, that deacon would have been removed from his position and probably sent packing. But this church was at a financial crossroads, on the edge of bankruptcy, and this chairman was a major contributor responsible for a hefty percentage of the church's income. So the church looked the other way. His affair was public, out for all to see, but the church carried on like nothing had happened, all for the sake of keeping their doors open. They kept the rot festering for financial well-being. That church was collectively, as one body, a sinner in need of a Savior, but to our knowledge, they never repented. They never accepted the invitation to the revival, and even if they had, they never saw their own need for Jesus. Just the need for more money. That's not an ekklesia of Christ. That's a sinkhole of sin.

That's why it's so important to admit you are a sinner. It's not enough for your sin to be public, like the deacon's. Your need for a Savior has to be public too. Openly committing evil isn't being vulnerable. It's being vile. Instead, openly professing that you have sinned and need some rescuing force to redeem you is a step on the path toward wholeheartedness. Individuals must do this, and therefore many churches must as well. They need to personally accept their need for Jesus and then do so corporately, as well. The church is like a body, and it operates as a whole unit. When one part of it is infected, the whole body is at risk. Therefore, the whole body must do something about it. We're not talking about more committees, more structures, or more programming. And we're certainly not talking about more shame. We're talking about transparency, vulnerability, and repentance. We're talking about change.

So yes, many churches need to admit that they need Jesus far more than they realize. What comes after that is equally important. Do you believe that Jesus is your Savior and Lord? Even for churches, this is rough. Those words are heavy with implications. The first keyword to break down is *believe*. For many people, that means a mental assent to a set of principles or commands, but biblically speaking, it's so much more than that. It's about being persuaded deep down in your soul to the point of total surrender. It means to trust with your life. Faith is not about thinking a certain rock is a good handhold. It's about actually reaching for that rock and putting your full weight on it.

Most churches don't do that because most people don't do that. Most churches think that if they gather up enough funding, they don't need Jesus to come through for them. If they can just sing the right songs, pray the right prayers, hire the right pastors, and listen to the right sermons, all in the right order, that they don't require Jesus to be their Savior. But, as one pastor friend of ours is fond of doing, we recommend those churches go to a graveyard and stand by a tomb. They should then ask themselves this question: What church strategy, song, sermon, fundraiser, or practice can raise a body out of its grave?

None. Only Jesus can do that. So it's necessary for churches to believe, not in themselves or their capabilities, but in Christ as the only rock that can hold them up on the cliffside. Only Jesus can save. Only Jesus can redeem. Only Jesus can atone. We can't do it on our own. Churches, evangelical ones, in particular, are so fond of preaching the doctrine of total depravity, wherein we're all sinners who can't save ourselves, but they tend to act as if they collectively can. If they can just find the right combination of holy practices and present a righteous front for long enough, then they think they are their own saviors. They try to pull themselves up by their bootstraps, only to find themselves barefoot.

Jesus must become to churches their only Savior. It's not enough to sing about it. We have to live like it's true. In the same way, he must also be our Lord. That's not an everyday word in American English except in churches, so let's break it down. It means "Master" or, better yet, "Owner." With that definition in mind, it's not enough for us to preach about Jesus, or to have crosses hanging in our buildings, or even to agree with his teachings. He has to be the Boss, the Master, and the Owner. As Paul writes, "He is the head of the body, the church; he is the beginning and the firstborn from among the dead, so that in everything he might have the supremacy" (Colossians 1:18).

Supremacy. Again, that's not a common English word, but the Greek word there is otherwise translated as "first place" (*New American Standard Bible*). Jesus is given the highest award, the position of honor, not only in name but also in command. He is the one to submit to. He is the one to obey. He is the one to follow. He is Lord.

That means we have to stop debating his teachings and instead live as if they were true. He says not to judge, so we have to stop, even when we think we're right. He says to pray for our enemies, even though they make our blood boil and we think we know better. He says to care for our neighbor, even when we think they don't deserve it and have brought their ruin upon themselves. He says not to call names, not to harbor bitterness, and not to live in anger, lust, or self-righteousness. He says to pray in private and not to make a show of your piety. He says to do good deeds in secret and to expose instead your sins and your scars. He says to love each other and let that love speak its witness to a lost and lonely world. He says to go and make disciples, not to sit and make snarky comments.

Jesus is the Master. Jesus is the Owner. Jesus is the King. Churches must live as if that is true or else admit that they aren't churches at all. That requires us to honestly assess where we stand if we truly follow him. It requires continual repentance, a permanent revolution against self-seeking. It means communal contrition and corporate sorrow over our sins so they may be forgiven, and we can again rejoice. It will hurt. It will agonize. It will scar. But as King David tells us, God's "anger lasts only a moment, but his favor lasts a lifetime; weeping may stay for the night, but rejoicing comes in the morning" (Psalm 30:5).

In order to get to that joy, to reach that consolation, we must go through the tough, slow, painful night of repentance in confessing that Jesus is Savior and Lord. We must admit that we can't save ourselves and that following Jesus means a total commitment and obedience to what he has called us to. But that calling is not a burden. It doesn't weigh heavy, and it does not constrain unnecessarily. As Jesus says, "Come to me, all you who are weary and burdened, and I will give you rest. Take my yoke upon you and learn from me, for I am gentle and humble in heart, and you will find rest for your souls. For my yoke is easy and my burden is light" (Matthew 11:28–30).

We preach that constantly to people, hoping they will realize that Jesus is the only way forward. But we must accept that truth for ourselves or else remain under the burden of our sin forever.

The third question that commonly gets asked when you walk down the aisle at a revival is, Do you commit to following Jesus for all of your days? This one is hard too. It seems easy in the euphoric moment to say yes when your body is rushing with the feel-good hormones of serotonin and oxytocin. The adrenaline doesn't hurt, either. But when the mountaintop experience settles down and all those neurochemicals wear off, this is quite difficult to live out. It compels us to bring our sins out in the open daylight and watch them die. We tend to like sinning, and if it weren't for its disastrous consequences, we would probably like to go on sinning for as long as possible. Watching the habits you've spent decades developing die isn't fun, and it isn't easy. You'll want to dive in and save them from the fire, even at your own peril. It's like putting your photographs of a broken relationship in the dumpster. It may be necessary to move on, but it isn't at all pleasant. You will experience a longing the next time you choose not to go to a party because you've committed to following Jesus instead of pursuing revelry. You'll cry when you choose against an attractive man or woman because you know that pursuing that relationship will lead to lust instead of healthy intimacy. And you may even experience physical withdrawal symptoms when you give up an addiction like pornography, alcohol, or other drugs. It hurts to watch your sin die.

That's because the brain is a habit-forming machine. Every time it creates a new shortcut to its goals, it celebrates and shores up that shortcut so it's easier to reach the next time. That's why it's so easy to get hooked on certain behaviors, like when you use Netflix-binging, social media's infinite scroll, or alcohol consumption to deal with otherwise messy emotions like boredom, anxiety, and loneliness. Once you've found the shortcut out of those, your brain throws a party, and it commits itself to form a habit so you won't ever have to feel that way again. This leads to a functional addiction, and just like with any drug, it becomes a bandage you use to cover the gushing wounds you have inside your soul.

We are all addicted to sin because it's the easy way out of our desires. Bitterness is the easy way out of wanting a good relationship. Self-indulgence is the easy way out of wanting intimacy. Greed is the easy way out of wanting a comfortable life. Laziness is the easy way out of wanting rest. Sin is always the easy way out, and so our brains celebrate it when we find it because it shortcuts the distance to what we crave.

The problem arises when that shortcut doesn't allow us to pursue the healthy paths to those desires, and thus the result feels shallow and unfulfilling. The difficulty comes out because we become so accustomed to the shortcut that we tend to prefer it to the real thing. It's craving fast food over a well-prepared healthy dinner. It's longing for pornography over intimacy. It's yearning for an alcohol binge over spending a good time with friends or family. We all succumb to this notion, and the Bible has a good word for this feeling: *entangled* (see Hebrews 12:1).

So many people are entangled in sin today because they haven't given themselves fully over to the purifying power of pursuing Jesus. Likewise, many churches are also entangled. We're not making any implications about eternity here, but rather we are saying there are a great many churches that, as a whole, simply do not follow Jesus and have not committed to dealing with their sin. These are the churches that preach hostility, that live for arguments and disputes, that seek power and pride over penitence, and that pursue tradition as a substitute for faith. If a church's tone is more bitter than it is compassionate, if its message is more about brimstone than grace, if its fellowship is more about self-aggrandizing than self-awareness, then we argue that it's not a church at all. It needs to undergo a radical transformation, just as if it were a wayward sinner. It needs to come to the revival, repent, and then change forever.

Churches have been preaching that truth forever, but so rarely do we turn that lens back on ourselves as a mirror that we may not even recognize ourselves. So many of us have become destitute, festering, and pestilent, and we often don't realize it. That's what the world is rejecting. Not Jesus or his message of salvation, which they so desperately need. No, they've rejected us. Our bickering. Our in-fighting. Our hypocrisy. Our judgments. Our power-lust. Jesus didn't push them out. *We* did.

And so a radical transformation is required, a total refit. Maybe it would behoove your church to close its doors for a while and figure things out. Maybe it should dissolve for good, never having been a true ekklesia in the first place. Maybe it needs to get all its entangling sin out in the open so those habits can perish. Whatever the case, the only right response to a revival is a profound metamorphosis that changes us forever. It's not just heaven or hell that's on the line. It's our present lives, our ability to go on, and our sense of self. All that hangs in the balance.

Element #4: Inviting Others

But any good revival doesn't stop with just one person's transformation. Almost like a virus, the revival expects that transformed person to bring more people back to be transformed. Revivals are multiple nights in a row for a reason. If you've been affected by the good news, the best thing for you to do—really, the only thing for you to do—is to spread that good news to others. If you've been radically transformed by something, the first thing anybody does is talk about it. Whether it's the diet that finally worked for you, the new exercise that you learned, or finding the love of your life, you're going to tell everyone you know. Not just out of a sense of duty or social guilt, but because it's the biggest thing on your mind and heart. You want other people to go through what you've gone through and to experience what you've experienced. Keeping it to yourself isn't an option because it's just too good not to share.

In the same way, churches must obsess over sharing the good news about Jesus. That doesn't mean invading their lives to bring about a constant sense of shame. Rather, that means disrupting the barriers between people and Jesus. It means accepting the mess in others' lives so when they ask you the way out, you point to Christ. It's not highlighting sin or giving it any more power than it already has over other people's lives. It's showing that sin can be defeated by uncovering it in our own lives and showing people how we have set it on fire. It's dying to sin over and over again so when people acknowledge your wholeheartedness and the freedom with which you walk, you can say honestly and earnestly that it was Christ who did the resurrecting.

There is no point in anyone's faith journey where the essential Gospel of Christ is not the most important aspect for growth. Are you going through depression? Jesus saves. Are you trapped by an addiction? Jesus saves. Are you caught in the throes of meaningless lust? Jesus saves. Are you enduring suffering or grief or agony because of your wrongdoing or someone else's? Jesus saves. Are you stuck being greedy or lazy or a liar? Jesus saves. That salvation is always the most crucial element for life change.

That's true individually and as a whole church. Churches must tell the Gospel week in and week out. It can't be an afterthought. It can't be hidden in the ritual. It must be first, middle, and last. The good news must permeate all of our elements: every song, every reading, every sermon, and every practice. We have to connect each spoke to the center of the wheel, or else we will disrupt what it means to be a church.

We have to constantly invite others into the process, or else what are we doing? We as authors have been to far too many church services that only invoked the Gospel at the tail end, if at all, with no real connection to what else had happened there. A whole sermon would go by explaining Jesus's miracle of changing water to wine, for example, with no mention of how Jesus had changed the pastor or anyone else in the same way. That's a golden opportunity wasted. On the off-chance that first-time guests who didn't know Jesus were there, they would exit (and likely never come back) never learning about his saving grace, never hearing about how his total life transformation is exactly what they've been looking for since the beginning of their lives.

Every Easter, most churches do a big push to get people to come to church. This is like May sweeps week for the networks. It's a big deal that lets you know how many people are actually interested in your church, and for many visitors, it's the one opportunity they have to ever really hear about Jesus. Churches go all out for this. They send out fliers; they give out invitation cards; they make splashy social media announcements. Some even take out local ads or rent out billboards. Signs litter yards for acres and acres. It's a big deal to churches that people attend.

Once the masses get there, they are positively bombarded with what that church thinks is essential. Usually, that means Gospel-centered music and messages. It certainly means producing excellence in all modes of communication and the environment. And it means a big push to get people to hear the good news about Jesus. Anything and everything is thought about from the perspective of the guests who rarely hear about the salvation of God so they may know Christ (or at least know that church can be fun).

So here's our question as authors: Why isn't this just as true in October as it is in April? Why are so many of our Sundays mundane and uninteresting? Why do we get so lost in the ritual of it that we forget the compelling strangeness of it? And why do we forget all about that guest's experience? True, many churches (particularly church plants) have responded to this, but even they have to admit that most of their attempts at relevance are still wrapped up in ritual, tradition, and routine. There's nothing wrong with that, so long as it's explained afresh every time it is conducted. By all means, take communion every Sunday. But explain its significance every time. It really doesn't take that long. ("The bread we eat and the juice we drink remind us of the sacrifice Jesus made to forgive us of our sins." See? One sentence is all it took.) If you want to read liturgy each week, that's fine too. (That's what hymns and songs are, after all.) Just explain upfront to your guests how to participate and what's expected of them. Do you want to sing about the blood of Jesus? By all means, do so. That's good news. But don't do so in a vacuum or in a way that only Christians can understand. Explain what you mean as if you've never heard it before.

In this way, we should always be inviting. We're not asking people to join a ritual, after all. We're asking them to participate in total life transformation, just like the one we've been through. We can't pretend that what we do or believe is normal. It's not. It's fascinatingly different. And if it isn't, you're not doing it right. Even the most normal churches out there are still doing a mashup of a rock concert, karaoke, a TED talk, and a snack. That's weird. Let it be weird. But don't let it go unexplained. Continue to invite people deeper into the process of setting their sins on fire so they can be free of their entanglement.

Once people go through this revival, nothing is allowed to be the same. They should talk differently, walk differently, and live differently. The same thing is true of churches. Once they've accepted the invitation, gone through the Gospel crisis, and been radically transformed, they have to invite others to do the same. Christianity has no room for lone wolves. We're just not given that option, biblically or practically. What we do must be done in community. But for that to be a community worth joining, it has to be one of constant revival.

Further Questions

1. If you've ever been to a church event, why did you go?
2. What has been your experience with accepting invitations to church events like services, camps, or revivals? Was it good? Bad? Ugly? What made it those things?
3. Have you ever been through a Gospel crisis moment where your life was laid out in front of you and you were compelled to make a change? What did you do? Why?
4. Have you ever been through or seen a church go through a radical transformation? What did that look like? What changed? How long did it last?
5. What would it take for a church to be truly inviting to people who don't already go there? What would it have to do?

11

---◆---

The Party That Didn't Go So Well

It was supposed to be a normal party. Everyone had worn their good clothes and was on their best behavior. They were all reclining at the table with ceremonially washed feet and hands. The bread in particular was excellent. It happened to be a Saturday lunch, on what the Jews there considered the Sabbath day, a day of rest. They had been told hundreds of generations ago not to work on the Sabbath out of special reverence to God. It was a sign since their time of wandering in the desert that they trusted God for their provision.

Some people had gotten together in the last couple of centuries or so and decided for themselves (and for many others) what it meant to work on such a day. You could only walk so far, touch so many things, eat certain kinds of food because they didn't require work on the day of the Sabbath itself, and so on. Most especially, you couldn't do anything stressful or meaningful with your everyday job. This was a ritual day of rest, and you were supposed to honor that.

That's certainly why Jesus and the people at this party were mostly eating bread. Bread could keep from the day before and didn't require any work on the day of its consumption. And this wouldn't be just any bread. It would almost definitely have been *matzah*, unleavened bread, in honor of the Israelites' famous Passover meal. The religious elites with whom Jesus was celebrating the Sabbath would have eaten nothing else.

The story we're told includes a little detail. It says that Jesus "was being carefully watched" (Luke 14:1), almost like he would steal something. The Pharisees knew Jesus well enough to know that he loved to heal people and that he had no problem doing so, regardless of the day of the week. He had done it before, and he would do it again. So they set up a little trap for him by inviting a man with "abnormal swelling of the body" (v. 2), or dropsy, just to see what Jesus would do.

Think about that for the man with the swelling. There he was with a debilitating illness, probably unable to walk without great effort. He had certainly violated the Sabbath just to get there because all his movements would have been labored. The Pharisees and experts in the Jewish law probably looked down on him for his heavy breathing, thinking he had broken a significant religious rule. Honoring the Sabbath, after all, was one of the Big Ten, right alongside worshipping God alone and not murdering anyone. According to these religious elites, helping someone on the Sabbath was as bad as killing them any other day of the week. But there this man was, heaving with great effort, only to be used as a pawn in their political game.

Jesus, as he was fond of doing, decided to make a show of this situation and embarrass the Pharisees. This man with dropsy was clearly suffering. He had even committed a grave crime just by getting himself there. The Pharisees had planned this as a test for Jesus, but now that they saw the ill man, they perhaps pitied him. So Jesus asks a question: "Is it lawful to heal on the Sabbath or not?" (v. 3).

This turned the trap on its head. Surely, the Sabbath was meant for rest, and rest implied that even doctors take the day off. But no one was supposed to suffer needlessly on the Sabbath either, right? After all, isn't suffering in itself a kind of work? Should they look down on people for their pain and refuse to help them just because of a religious rule, even a big one? Jesus's question left the Pharisees in befuddled silence. Staring slack-jawed at the sick man, they had no answer. Their trap for Jesus had become a snare for their conscience, and they found themselves bewildered by their own plan.

This scenario has played out in churches all across the United States for decades. We pay homage to the rules of our religion, by which we mean tithing, church attendance, and trying not to cuss. But when we come across someone in agony, someone in dire need of assistance, we're often left stupefied because it never occurs to us not to look down on them until they are right in front of us. And here, we're not talking just about the sick. Churches are actually surprisingly good at caring for the physical needs of their members. No, we're talking about the spiritually sick, the people who have abnormally swollen souls and are carrying around so much baggage that they spread their sense of burden to anyone they meet. They cry at our songs when they're not supposed to. They weep at our sermons about conscience and sin. They wail in our small groups when they hear the reading of scripture. They just won't play it cool. They aren't playing the same game we are. We came to what we thought was a club because we wanted our Jesus-fix and to move on for the week. They came to what they thought was a hospital because they were bleeding to death. We're playing dress-up on Sunday mornings. They're dying.

And we simply don't know what to do with them. They force us to see brokenness in them, and so we are compelled to see brokenness in ourselves. All of our rituals mean nothing if we're not devastated at the sight of them, but we simply have no response to their situation. So Jesus asks us the same thing he asked the Pharisees: Is it lawful to heal on the Sabbath or not?

We would so much rather that our Sunday mornings go on uninterrupted by these people's blubbering. Walk in, shake hands, sing, sit, listen, stand, sing, pray, leave. That's what we want to happen at 10 a.m. We want to be out in time to not have to wait long for lunch. But these people take our rituals and turn them on their head. We have unspoken rules about how things are supposed to go, but we often let those rules guide our behaviors in ways that oppress people's souls. We quiet them down instead of letting them speak their consciences. We try to calm them instead of joining them in their repentance. We escort them out the rear door when they cry out to God (we authors have seen this happen) instead of standing beside them and praying with them.

Is it lawful to heal on the Sabbath or not?

"So taking hold of the man, he healed him and sent him on his way" (v. 4). Jesus decided to act. And so should we. We are called to nothing less than the total restoration of such people. They are examples to us, not we to them. They show us the way to repentance and life change. They show us how to follow Jesus with all of our hearts and souls. They show us how to submit our sinful patterns to God for healing. We put on our Sunday best, whether that means our nicest clothing or our happiest smiles, but these people show us what church is supposed to look like. The church isn't a hangout; it's a hospital. We can provide all the free coffee and excellent service we want, but if our churches are not places for the healing of the brokenhearted, then they're not churches at all. We can't reject these people, for then we have rejected ourselves.

Jesus asks the Pharisees there, "If one of you has a child or an ox that falls into a well on the Sabbath day, will you not immediately pull it out?" (v. 5). In our context, we ask this question a little differently. If your child is depressed, will you not sit and cry with them instead of forcing them to put on their best Sunday smile? If your sibling is transgender, will you not stand next to them on a Sunday morning and accept the awkward stares with them? If your father is going through a messy divorce, will you not sit beside him in the small group anyway? If your sister is forcing herself to throw up on Saturday nights, would you still want her with you at the church potluck on Sunday afternoon? If your husband has cheated, if your daughter has given up her virginity, if your son has become addicted to pornography, if your mother has gambled away her life savings, or if your wife drinks a whole bottle of wine every day, are they still your family? Would you still want them at church with you?

Sadly, many people would choose against those people, even their own family. We've done it too. We'd rather keep up appearances. Sure, those people are welcome to come with us, as long as they behave themselves and dress appropriately and never mention any of those things. That's exactly the hypocrisy Jesus was calling out when he healed this sick man. He asks us the same question today: Would you not immediately pull them out? Would we not want them to experience the grace of Jesus as you have? Or must they clean themselves up first? Must they pull themselves out of the well before we will reach out a hand to them? Or are we so full of ourselves that we can't stand to have sinners and spiritually sick people around us?

Jesus then tells a little parable about how to get honored by humbling yourself, which we won't delve into here. It's what he says next that leaves our jaws on the floor: "When you give a luncheon or dinner, do not invite your friends, your brothers or sisters, your relatives, or your rich neighbors" (v. 12).

That goes totally against our sensibilities of how we should invite people to church. We typically think we're supposed to reach inside our inner circles and see who will bite on the invitation. There's an extent to which that's true, but Jesus tells us to go beyond our normal groups. We shouldn't invite people to church who already have it all together, who already live good lives, and who already fit our standard of what it means to be one of us. If they own the right clothes, smile the right way, and have a stiff upper lip, don't invite them. If they act appropriately, have their life in order, and present a good front, don't invite them. These are the people in a position to do your church a favor and to make you look good. These are the people you want at church because they make everyone feel good and comfortable, especially if they tithe well.

Jesus gives an alternative. "But when you give a banquet, invite the poor, the crippled, the lame, the blind" (v. 13). Jesus says to invite the very people who can't repay you, who don't make you look good, and who make you uncomfortable. Jesus says to invite the people who will act out, the people who don't get it, and the people who won't dress the right way. They spiritually stink of their sin, and they don't know how to mask it with penitent perfume. They behave awkwardly, they wear the wrong clothes, and they don't know instinctively when to stand, sit, sing, or stay silent. They're a mess.

But that mess belongs in the church. Not only because they need us, but more so because we need them. Yes, they need Jesus to rescue them, but that only reminds us of our need to be rescued as well. They need a spiritual deep cleanse, but so do we. They need to "work out [their] salvation with fear and trembling" (Philippians 2:12), but so do we. Having these people around not only benefits them, but it compels us to continue coming back to the essential Gospel over and over again. We so often think that if we insulate ourselves with holy people that we'll become holier ourselves, but we have it backwards. In the same way that working with the sick makes one a better doctor, surrounding ourselves with sinners makes us better Christians. Sometimes, it's tempting to join them in their sin. That's a problem, yes. But if we remain steadfast by accepting them for who they are while we also show them the way out of their sinful patterns, we find the way out of ours as well. Cushioning your soul only with holy people who are already like you doesn't strengthen you. It atrophies you. But exposing yourself to the real world works out the muscles of your soul, enabling you to run toward Jesus and to lift the sick and dying toward him, as well.

Jesus makes one more important note here about these people, though. He says, "Although they cannot repay you, you will be repaid at the resurrection of the righteous" (v. 14). They cannot repay you. That means we won't necessarily get anything out of the experience of inviting the sin-entangled to our church. They can't or won't necessarily tithe well. They probably won't join the choir. They may not speak up in Sunday school or read their Bibles. They may not even believe in Jesus or get baptized. They may never do anything for us in any sense that serves to repay us for letting them join us. But Jesus says we should invite them anyway. Again, not as a favor to them or to hold ourselves in high regard for being ultra-Christian. But because we run hospitals, not health spas. We're medics on the battlefield, not plastic surgeons in a cozy operating room. We're not about making people look better. We're about saving lives from destruction. If we can't get behind that mission, if we can't see ourselves to that duty, then it's in question whether or not we believe what we say we believe. It's in question whether we've been healed ourselves. Just because we look healthy on the outside doesn't mean we aren't gangrenous on the inside.

Once Jesus said that, the dinner party was effectively over. No one was smiling. They were barely even eating anymore. You could have heard the children playing in the street outside. One man decided to speak up to break the tension by saying something that sounded holy. "Blessed is the one who will eat at the feast in the kingdom of God" (v. 15).

Isn't that just what we do when things get awkward at church? We say all sorts of things that sound righteous and wonderful on the outside but have almost no meaning whatsoever. Things like "God has a plan," or "Everything happens for a reason," or (our personal favorite) "This is just a season in your life." What good do those statements do? Even if they happen to be true (they're usually not, at least not in the way we mean them), these clichés offer nothing to people who desperately need help. When we speak like this, we become hapless to people who are hopeless. It comforts no one but ourselves. It's an attempt at piety without compassion.

Jesus completely ignored this man's statement and instead went into a parable about another banquet. In his story, the master of the banquet first invited a great many important guests. But one after another, they each have an excuse for not coming. One of them had just bought a new property. Another had just purchased oxen for his work and had to test them out. Still another had just gotten married and thus declined. So the servant who sent out the invitations came back to the master of the banquet and told him all this. "Then the owner of the house became angry and ordered his servant, 'Go out quickly into the streets and alleys of the town and bring in the poor, the crippled, the blind and the lame'" (v. 21).

Jesus invites us to realize the kind of invitation he has handed out. So many of us are so busy trying to look the right way, do the right thing, and play the holy game that we ignore the party that is supposed to be happening in our midst. We were invited, but we have given excuse after excuse as to why we can't come. Maybe we're too rich, like the person who just bought the property. Maybe we're too career-obsessed, like the person who just bought the oxen for his work. And maybe we're too concerned with our own families, like the one who just got married. Whatever the case, we've declined the invitation. We look like we have it all together, and all the pieces of our lives are well constructed. But we've ignored the invitation to the party our God is trying to throw. He wants our attention, and we've spurned him.

Lest you think this is other people, have you truly accepted the invitation? We talked in the last chapter about attending the revival. Have you come? Have you gone through the Gospel crisis? Have you been radically transformed? Is your life substantially different now that you've decided to follow Jesus? Or is it just the same old thing? Are you still playing dress-up on Sunday mornings and pretending it's a solemn event? Or are you ready for the party?

So God invites instead "the poor, the crippled, the blind and the lame" (v. 21). The people who don't get it. Who can't get it. The people who don't understand and never will. The people who sing in the wrong key, who sin in the wrong way, who believe the wrong things, and who act like they don't have anything to lose. Because they don't.

God welcomes the very people the original invitees would have rejected. He goes on a recruiting mission to lavish his love upon the hurting and the helpless. And when his servant says that "what you ordered has been done, but there is still room" (v. 22), God invites still more to the table, ordering that servant to "go out to the roads and country lanes and compel them to come in, so that my house will be full" (v. 23). God sends out the servant to the open country, to the outskirts of civilization, to those who would never have even gotten an invitation in the first place, all for the sake of filling his home with celebration.

This would have been the party of the year, but Jesus gave a stern warning: "I tell you, not one of those who were invited will get a taste of my banquet" (v. 24). Not one. This means that if we're those people who are already on the inside of the right social circle, who already dress the right way and know the right people, we still only get one shot, just like everybody else. God invites everyone in this story to his feast, but he rejects those who reject him from the outset. If we're stuck in our ways, if we've got better things to do with our time, if we've got our lives to live, then there's no room for us at his table. In the same way, if we wouldn't show up to his party because of who's there, we don't belong.

That's what Jesus was saying to the Pharisees. They had missed the point of their religiosity. They were so busy following rules and keeping themselves ritually pure that they forgot what their faith practice was all about. It wasn't a set of rituals. It was the seeking of justice, mercy, humility, and compassion. Every Pharisee there would have known the following words: "He has shown you, O mortal, what is good. And what does the LORD require of you? To act justly and to love mercy and to walk humbly with your God" (Micah 6:8), "for I desire mercy, not sacrifice, and acknowledgment of God rather than burnt offerings" (Hosea 6:6).

The Pharisees had gone out of their way to sacrifice in all the right ways. They had followed all the rules, completed all the rituals, and fulfilled all the requirements, just like so many American Christians have done. We kept sex for marriage. We attended church every Sunday for decades. We abstained from drugs. We never got drunk. We didn't cuss (well, hardly ever). We covered our bodies modestly. We practiced communion. We tithed. We did all the things we thought we were supposed to do—except what God really wanted. God wants our attitudes, not just our actions. He wants our identities, not just our good deeds. He wants our souls, not just our sacraments. He wants us.

God wants love. He wants compassion. He wants justice and mercy. He wants self-sacrifice. He wants us to submit to others and to accept the consequences of our actions. He wants actual righteousness, not apparent righteousness. Everything else is what Jesus calls "whitewashed tombs, which look beautiful on the outside but on the inside are full of the bones of the dead and everything unclean" (Matthew 23:27). And it's there that we have to pay attention. What Jesus calls churches to is nothing short of admitting their spiritual death. He doesn't want another pious deed, another good ritual, or another new song. He wants that death to come out of us. He wants to resurrect us.

That takes work. It takes an honest assessment and a total capitulation. This means that churches can't fake it any longer, nor can we expect anyone else to. The church needs to become what Pastor Timothy Keller calls "a community of profound consolation, a place where you get enormous support for suffering and where people find themselves growing, through their troubles, into the persons God wants them to become" (*Walking with God through Pain and Suffering*, p. 193). That means being real, open, and honest. That means being true to our calling by being true to ourselves and Christ. That means going through the hard work of actually giving our sins over to Jesus.

Those things don't happen easily, nor by accident, but it's the only way forward. It's the only way out of the well. Thankfully, Jesus heals on the Sabbath, even when he's not supposed to. He can resurrect us back to life. He can breathe new oxygen into our lungs and revive us. That doesn't just apply to those who have hit rock bottom on a personal level. It applies also to churches that have done so on a corporate level. When we realize that we're just as lost as everyone else, just as desperately in need of Jesus, that's when we start to hear the servant's invitation to the Master's party. When we accept that we are just as poor, crippled, blind, and lame when it comes to sin as the rest of the world, we can recognize that the feast to which we're invited is where we want to be. We'll forsake our wealth. We'll give up our jobs. We'll even put our families on the back burner. Everything becomes about pursuing Jesus for all he's worth, which is everything.

So maybe Jesus needs to interrupt our perfect little Sunday gatherings, just like he interrupted this Sabbath meal with the Pharisees. Maybe he needs to get in our face about what we believe and what we hold dear to show us that what we think matters doesn't at all. Maybe he needs to remind us of the poor, crippled, blind, and lame, not so we can be their savior, but so we can recognize that we're among them, just as hopeless without Jesus as they are. Our good deeds and right doctrines do nothing more to save us than our suits, ties, dresses, and bonnets. Nothing we do can resurrect the dead from the grave. Nothing we do can bring buried souls back to life. Only Jesus saves them, and only Jesus can save us.

Further Questions

1. What has been your typical church experience? What normally happens on Sunday mornings? What about it is good? What about it seems fake or phony?
2. What people do you know who desperately need hope? What can you do for them?
3. How have you judged other people unnecessarily? How have you contributed to the rejection of people Jesus has invited to the party?
4. What in your life is poor, crippled, blind, or lame? How can you deal with that?

12

The Bride

When you were growing up, you probably went to a school of some kind. Only about 3 percent of students are fully homeschooled, so communal schooling is a shared experience that nearly all of us have. In school, we're placed in a unique working environment where everyone shares mostly the same goals and obstacles. You may have a snotty teacher, but so does the kid sitting next to you. Math may be tough for you, but it's the same test for everybody. And most of all, you're in a social pressure cooker of sorts. You spend day in and day out with the same people for hours and hours each week. You celebrate birthdays and holidays together, you share goals and outcomes, and you experience growth together.

There's nothing quite like it. Later work experiences don't mirror it very well, as people tend to come and go there quite frequently and are in different stages of life. It's no wonder that so many of us look back fondly at our school experiences. We shared everything with those people. They knew us, and we knew them. We practiced vulnerability and learned from our mistakes together. These people saw you at your absolute silliest (what else is middle school, after all?), but most people find some good friends during this time, sometimes for life. What else compares to this?

The church. Though it doesn't have all of the same elements, many people grew up in the church with a similar environment to school. There were shared beliefs, shared practices, shared experiences, and shared goals. We strove together, ate together, sat together, served together, and sang together. We even went to camps and slept in the same rooms together. We were vulnerable. It was wonderful.

Until somebody messed it up. They took advantage of you. They didn't like you. They didn't listen to you. They laughed at your eagerness to learn. And they didn't take you seriously when you had grown-up questions because they knew you when you were in diapers. They gave canned answers and quasi-religious nonsense, and they ended up hurting you for being different. Why would you ever want to go back?

Well, because church, at least when it's done right, can be an ideal community. The same people who wouldn't listen to your questions would gladly sit by your bedside at a hospital and pray for you. The same people whose religiosity made you mad would likely come to your mother's funeral and pay their respects. The same people you thought didn't like you would at least pay homage to the idea of loving you. Church has a lot of mass to it and therefore a lot of gravity. When its inertia is channeled poorly, it spins out of control and throws everyone off alone into the cosmos. Asteroids crash into people's lives, and planets slam into one another.

But when the church's inertia is channeled in a healthy way, the orbits it establishes are really quite extraordinary. It loves without question. It shows compassion. It throws shame off you instead of onto you. It casts out fears. It models itself based on love. It cares for its neighbors. It heals relationships. It reconciles divisions. And it doesn't scare easily. The church can be the best experience you'll ever have.

How do you find such a church? What do you look for? That's what a later chapter is all about, but first, we have some work to do on you. We've taken a hard drill to the American church's teeth, but it's time we took one to our own. Because as much as we'd love to blame the church for all of our spiritual problems, the truth is that we all bear at least some portion of the responsibility.

We know of one pastor who does a great deal of marital counseling. In his sessions, he'll draw a circle and ask one of the parties how much of the current problem is their fault compared to how much is the other person's fault. Invariably, the person draws a relatively small wedge, say 15 or 20 percent of the circle. Whatever the amount is, the pastor says, "Great. That's how much you need to own." Whatever that person's share of the responsibility is, that's what they need to learn how to grow through.

The same thing applies to our church experience. The church may have done a great amount of harm to us. You may only be responsible for a minuscule percentage of what went on there. It could just be that you stayed quiet when you shouldn't have and silently slipped out the back door instead of dealing with the issue. It really could be that small. Let's say that your fault in your church experience is just 5 percent. The rest of the church bears 95 percent of the blame, which is why we as authors have been taking it to task for the last several chapters. They're the ones who failed you 95 percent of the time while you were the victim, and you only carry 5 percent of the burden for what went down.

That's your 5 percent. Own it.

This is so important in our relationships. If you're married, you've got to own your piece of the pie too. This is no different. No matter how toxic the relationship has been (almost), you bear at least some smidgeon of the responsibility. We don't say this to shame you. We say this to awaken you. The church may have done 95 percent of the damage, and you therefore may think that your

5 percent is minuscule. But your 5 percent matters. Yes, the church did a lot of shoving to get you to leave, but in most cases, you were the one who decided never to give any other church a try because of that experience. You conflated your church with every church and decided to reject all of them.

It's not up to us to scold you for never going back to church. That's your call. We only hope that you'll realize what church can be: a life-defining community experience. That's what it was when you were a child, not only because you were young and impressionable, but also because you forged meaningful relationships and shared your journey toward worthwhile goals. There's a risk in that—there's always a risk in that, even outside of church—but we think it's worth the risk of getting hurt again.

We speak from experience.

Daniel briefly touched on his adult church experience in the preface. If you didn't read it because you're like us and always skip the prefaces of books, go back and read it now. Just dog-ear this page and come back. We'll wait.

Done? Okay.

You'll notice that Daniel talked a little bit about the churches he and his wife found on their way to a truly wonderful church home in Maryland. The circumstances behind them looking for a church were less than ideal. Daniel had worked in a ministry position in the church where he and his wife first met, but due to a significant lapse in his moral judgment, he blew up his ministry career. That church told him never to set foot on their property again. Was that the right decision on their part? Probably not. But Daniel certainly owned a piece of the guilt pie.

Either way, Daniel and his future wife were left looking for churches in the worst possible circumstance, knowing no one and having little hope. They found their way to a church that had a great homelessness ministry and was led with seeming compassion, except for the rampant sin of some of its leaders. They were so popular among their parishioners, though, that they simply didn't hold them accountable. Their denomination ultimately discharged them, but the church went on as if nothing had changed. That was, after all that effort, not the place for Daniel and his future wife, who went looking for healing elsewhere.

They wound up at a nondenominational community church where they met two lifelong friends. This church was fairly typical in its approach. Medium-sized with a good young adult group who all seemed to like each other well enough. A little too well. As it turns out, those people had all known each other for the better part of twenty years, having grown up in that church together. Many of them were even related by either marriage or blood. These people conveniently forgot to invite Daniel and his future wife to group events, and they didn't seem to enjoy it much when they showed up. Except for one friendship, nothing came of going to that church, so Daniel and his future wife left.

That's when Daniel wrote the letter he talked about in the preface, thinking it was all the church's fault that he felt so distant from God. Yes, he had blown up his opportunity to lead. That was his fault. But he also felt completely burned by the churches that followed. He and his wife kept looking, but it was years of searching and heartbreak before they found that one church in Maryland where everything changed. Years of pain, agony, and grief. Years of deconstructing and reconstructing what faith looked like for them. And what's worse, when they moved to Florida for career purposes, the same thing happened again. Churches and their leaders continued to disappoint, and Daniel and his wife spent years trying to find a true home.

But they wouldn't trade those years for the world.

Yes, they were hurt. Yes, they were bruised. Yes, they suffered. But through that adversity, they met themselves in whole new ways. It was miserable to the point of giving up entirely, but they didn't. They kept coming back. They kept committing and serving and trying. And they would say it's all been worth it. God was there for them in those times, even when all hope had been snuffed out, and in the cold darkness, they found the warmth of God's provision. It wasn't easy, and it's not even necessarily over, but it's been rewarding every step of the way. They have grown into themselves and matured in their faith, all because they didn't give up.

That's what seeking after a church can do. Even if you never find what feels like home again (it's hard, as we'll explore in the next chapter), the process is worth it. Jesus has found Daniel and his wife in the dark recesses between churches so many times, and each time, he has picked them back up, dusted them off, and set them out to love his church again.

In Lori's case, hurt came in many different forms. There were times when she felt the sting of ostracism and judgment from a church body, but it landed differently in her heart and mind. To say she is an optimist is an understatement. She is the worst poker player ever, not because she can't reason or bluff, but because she believes every hand has potential. The same thing happened to her with churches, where she would feel discouraged or disappointed but the feelings would eventually rally to a great "yeah, but what if" justification, thinking that each new day brought with it a new potentiality. This set her up to get burned again and again and again. She believes down to her feet that God so loved the church that he gave and because he thought we were worth it, junk and all. Lori believes that anything, any hand, is capable of redemption in the Jesus economy, and so she is compelled to stay working in messy churches for the sake of the Gospel. She wants to be a part of the change that God requires of us, the hope, love, and grace of the Gospel for all.

You see, whether you want to believe it or not, Jesus loves the American church, even at its worst. It may continue to play the harlot, but he has never given up on it. Earlier in the book, we compared the American church to ancient Israel, saying it has committed idolatry and largely given up on loving Jesus. Again, that's not true of each church, but it is a pattern across the American church as a whole. The American church has been idolatrous for generations now, but have you read what God said to the Israelites, whom he also called idolatrous?

> "I will punish her for the days she burned incense to the [idols]; she decked herself with rings and jewelry, and went after her lovers, but me she forgot," declares the LORD. (Hosea 2:13)

Okay, so God is going to punish the Israelites for their continued idolatry. Maybe the same thing will happen to the church. What's that going to look like?

> "Therefore I am now going to …" (v. 14)

Here it comes. Here comes the punishment. Here comes what we've all been waiting for, what we've all been hoping for. Here comes the judgment, the wrath, the fire and brimstone.

> "… allure her." (v. 14)

Wait, what? God, did you get that right? They hurt you. They spurned you. They chased after idols and rejected you. What do you mean you're going to allure them? How can this be? Maybe we've got it wrong. Maybe it's a trick of some kind. Maybe he's just trying to lure Israel and the American church into a false sense of security before pulling the rug out from under them.

> "I will lead her into the wilderness …" (v. 14)

Okay, that seems to be setting up the trap. The wilderness is a pretty good place to get rid of the body. What is he going to do there exactly?

> "… and speak tenderly to her." (v. 14)

Wait, what? Hold on. Let's check the ledger here. What does that word *tenderly* mean? Maybe it's like a hushed whisper before he sinks in the knife of his wrath. Let's look it up. It's the Hebrew word *leb*, meaning "heart." So it could be translated as "speak to her heart." That doesn't sound very wrathful. Is this even the same God of the Old Testament? Where are the plagues, the meteors from the sky, and the floods? Wait, now we get it. Maybe he's going to finally have it out with Israel and the American church. "Speak to her heart" might mean that he's going to tell them all the things they've done wrong and let them have it.

> "There I will give her back her vineyards, and will
> make the Valley of [Trouble] a door of hope." (v. 15)

God, what are you doing? You're going to reward them? You're going to give them back what they wasted? Even though they totally blew it, you're going to restore them? Why? What sense does that make?

> "There she will respond as in the days of her youth,
> as in the day she came up out of Egypt." (v. 15)

Sorry, God, we just don't understand. What could you possibly want with Israel's or the American church's response? Unless, of course, what you want is obedience and love. Maybe you don't want to smite down your people. Maybe you really do want that relationship, not just with individuals but with the institution as a whole. Maybe when you called the church your bride, you meant it.

> "In that day," declares the LORD, "you will call
> me 'my husband'; you will no longer call me 'my
> master.'" (v. 16)

God doesn't even want to be called Master anymore. He wants to be called Husband. Here's where it gets a little bit technical, but that Hebrew word for "master" is *baal*, which also is the name of one of the idols Israel fell into worshipping, Baal. So when God declares that Israel will no longer call him Master, he's eliminating the word of the idol from their lips, even if its meaning pertains to him. In our context of the American church, this means we maybe should talk less about God's riches because we've worshipped greed. Maybe we should talk less about God's might since we've worshipped power. Maybe we should talk less about God being a King because we've worshipped our own political system. Instead, perhaps we should refer to this verse and talk about God's affection for us as a Husband, his pursuit of us in the wilderness, and his sacrificial compassion for us. That's certainly God's plan in the next verse.

> "I will remove the names of the [idols] from her lips;
> no longer will their names be invoked." (v. 17)

How will he do this? Not by coercion or force, and not by wrath, but by his tender lovingkindness. Many people today think God is out to get them for their sin, to trap them in their wrongdoing so he can exercise his anger on them. The American church has too often fed that narrative, but it's just not true. Yes, God wants to destroy sin and evil. But he's so much more gracious than he is angry. That applies to you, to us, to ancient Israel, and even to the American church. He wants reconciliation over wrath, and relationship over recompense. When it comes to the church in particular, do you know what God wants? A wedding.

> "I will betroth you to me forever; I will betroth
> you in righteousness and justice, in love and
> compassion. I will betroth you in faithfulness, and
> you will acknowledge the Lord." (vv. 19–20)

As much anger as God has toward the American church for our wrongdoing, his plan isn't to destroy us forever. He plans to reunite with us, to marry us. That's not us being worthy of it. That's him living out his covenant faithfulness. There's nothing we did to merit it. You may even think it awful that God would elevate such an institution to being his bride. But that's what he says he'll do.

We get that this is infuriating. It ticks us off too. It means that, as mad as we are, God operates in the spirit of forgiveness. As angry as we are and perhaps should be, God wants to redeem his people. After all, isn't that what we hope he'll do with each one of us? Don't we all long for reconciliation with the divine? Don't we all want to be saved by the tender mercy of a God who loves us? Why, then, should we want anything different for the American church? It's a broken, sinful mess. So are we all. But God restores.

Maybe you don't believe in God anymore. Maybe you want to sue him in court like Job wanted to do. Maybe you want nothing to do with him. But do you truly want to live forever in your contempt of the church? Is that the kind of person you want to become? Or do you, like God, have room in your heart for speaking tenderly, even to the one who maligned you?

Perhaps you'll never set foot in a church again. We think that's a tragedy, but we get it. Some churches are pretty awful. But what might it mean for you to give the Christian community an honest try? Might you search for just a little bit longer? Might you give God's bride just one more chance? He did, after all. Why not you?

You see, God is never done loving. Many of us think God is all about the long con, that all his talk about love and compassion is a bluff to get us to let our guard down and that all he wants is to smite us. But that gets lost in bad theology. God doesn't want to smite down evil people. He wants to smite down evil itself, evicting it from our hearts and souls so we can walk free of it. God doesn't want a world without us, but he does want a world without sin. The only reason we think God is after us is because of the perpetuated lie that we are sin. No, we're not. We're sinful. We're utterly entangled by its vines, which is why God wants to set those vines on fire. We'll get singed as they burn, but then we'll be free.

But the idea that we are sin is nonsense. Don't let anyone tell you differently. Sin is a force that must be reckoned with, so much so that Jesus died to disentangle us from it, but its power is not so great that it defines us. What does define us is God's proclamation that we are made in his image (see Genesis 1:27). That statement comes two whole chapters before sin enters the world, and that's important to remember. Too often, we get trapped into thinking that sin is our identity, but that's shame and death talking, not God. God wants to free us from the vines, and so he must set them on fire by his might. In this way, the wrath of God is good news.

God wants to do the same thing for the American church. He wants to set its entangling sin vines on fire in a controlled burn that deals with the problem without killing his bride. Even if you don't believe in God, you want that in your life too. You want to be free of your bad decision making, your addiction to choosing the wrong thing, and your frequent sense of shame and regret. You want to be free. We believe Jesus does that freeing, both for ourselves as individuals and for the church at large.

As Paul puts it, "Christ loved the church and gave himself up for her to make her holy, cleansing her by the washing with water through the word, and to present her to himself as a radiant church, without stain or wrinkle or any other blemish, but holy and blameless" (Ephesians 5:25–27). Jesus isn't full of animosity toward us, but rather compassion and affection. He doesn't call us to be holy because he is stingy or self-righteous, but because he knows that following after him is the best way to be truly free. He wants his bride to live her best life, and he invests in her ability to do so, to the point of death. Jesus does that for you, for us, and, yes, even for the American church. You may not think she is worthy of his love and forgiveness because of what she's done to her children. But God forgives even that grave sin.

You may think that's unjust or unfair, but so is all forgiveness. Every time we forgive someone, we are giving up our right to be angry, our right to wrath, and our right to bring about eternal judgment. Maybe that's where you are with the church, in a state of permanent conviction. You've sentenced the church for life, and you hope it rots in the prison of your soul. But in the same way God wants to set you free from sin, he also wants to set you free of bitterness. It's holding you back from being wholehearted. It's holding you back from being the loving force you wish the church had been in your life. It's holding you back from being free.

So maybe forgiveness is in order. Maybe forgiveness is the process you need to go through. You may never set foot in a church again, but you can find it in your heart to let go of your righteous outrage. Because God has.

Further Questions

1. Write down a list of names of people who hurt you at church. Specify how they hurt you and what the effects were on your life.

2. Yell at the names on the paper. Let them have it. Let it all out on the page. Be as angry as you want to be.

3. Now, how do you feel after having processed through that much rage? What emotions linger at the end of all that?

4. Looking at your list, whom do you need to forgive You don't necessarily have to reach out to them, let them know, or do anything awkward like that, but maybe you need to remove from your heart the bitterness you feel. Can you do that? How? What would be the effects?

13

Forgiving the Church

S o yes, it has to happen. You have to forgive the church. We'll try not to couch this in too religious of terms, but if you want to be free of the pain and damage the church has caused you, the only way forward is to untangle your heart from it. Whether or not you eventually go back to a church is your business, but we believe that, just like with a person who hurt you in the past, bitterness can't be the answer to a wholehearted life. You may never subject yourself to interacting with that person or church ever again, and that's okay, but forgiveness is the path forward to a better, freer existence.

We know this is hard. We know it's asking a lot. We realize that forgiveness bears with it the tendency to be set up to get hurt all over again. But if you're truly done with the church, if you really want it to no longer have that kind of gravitational hold on you, then like with a bad divorce, you have to forgive in order to move on. It may not be possible (or even advisable) for you to ever attend another church because of what happened to you there, but if you really want to say goodbye forever, then you have to be willing to let go of your right to be angry. Otherwise, you're drinking poison and hoping the other person dies.

On the flip side, maybe you want to go back to a church someday. That's great. We obviously want that for you because we think it can be an enormously positive experience. But before you walk through those doors, before you set yourself up to be vulnerable again, there's something you have to do: forgive the church. Yes, you too. You may be thinking that your willingness to go back illustrates that you've already done the forgiving, but watch yourself closely, or else you may just get hurt again. Continuing with the metaphor of a bad divorce, if you carry forward the pain, bitterness, and anger of your former relationship into the next one, all you'll do is poison the new marriage. It'll start off great because you think meeting a different person will alleviate all your ails, but then you'll catch yourself holding the previous spouse's deeds against the new one, being distrustful when they do things that remind you of your ex, and failing to be vulnerable when the relationship calls for it.

So you too need to forgive. It's not enough for you to simply go back. You have to undo the pain in your heart and burn off the entangling vines of agony and evil that defined your prior experience. Your church hurt you. It violated you. And until you deal with that and forgive that evil, you'll likely be trapped by it forever, even in a new church.

But how do we forgive the church when there's so much gall? How do we move forward and set ourselves free from the self-made prison of unforgiveness? According to many therapists, there are five steps. We'll cover them briefly here and then set you free to do the hard work of actually beginning the process of forgiveness.

Step 1: Acknowledge the Hurt

The first thing nearly everyone does when they start a forgiveness process is try to minimize the pain or deny the wrongdoing that hurt them. We talked about denial in an earlier chapter, and that's what we mean here. The kind of denial we discussed earlier, however, dealt with the pain itself, while this type deals with the person. Maybe you think the pain came from just that one church instead of the institution as a whole, so you think you can just go to another church and all will be well. This presents a serious problem in our thinking. We desperately want to feel safe, but after the trauma many have experienced in an American church, that kind of emotional security may not be possible without serious work to overcome the damage.

For one of us (Daniel), that meant he had to engage with what happened to him at church. He didn't meet with all the people who hurt him, and he didn't necessarily let them know that he was still hurt by what went on. But he did have to go through a process with a therapist and talk through what occurred so he could begin to heal. It was all too easy to minimize the pain and deny the wrong that was done to him, but in the end, Daniel realized that restoration would only occur if he named the pain.

It's also easy in this step to make excuses for the offender. In some cases, you really did have a part to play in what went down, and you need to make changes in your heart to make sure you don't behave that way again. But in many instances, we try to forgive the offending parties by pretending that mitigating circumstances made their actions acceptable. "They had the whole church to consider" is a common one when the hurt came from a pastor who ignored or belittled you. "It was best for everybody if I just left" is another common one when the hurt came from a particular group or the entire church. These can feel like forgiveness at first because you think you're being empathetic, but you're really just ignoring their error. That may make it feel better for a time, but it's not a permanent solution any more than ibuprofen cures a cut. It just numbs the pain for a little while. That cut doesn't (just) need pain medication; it needs a bandage.

It isn't until we come face to face with what actually hurt us that we can finally begin to heal. Knowing and admitting that you've got that cut is the first step in putting that bandage on it, and that requires us to fully come to terms with what caused it. In this case, the wound was inflicted on you by an institution (or its representative), and knowing how it hurt you is a meaningful step in resolving the tension. Toward that end, we recommend what is going to sound like a cliché at first, but we promise it helps: journaling.

Journaling serves to organize your thoughts and acknowledge the truth as you see it. Sometimes, writing a letter to the offenders is particularly helpful, though we recommend that you not necessarily send it. This aids you in exploring the issues at hand and provides you with a sense of clarity. For many people, just the act of writing it down is cathartic on its own, but we must advise here that this is not the last stage of forgiveness. It will feel good to get all your rage and pain out (we've written more than one letter like this, and it's always an emotional ride), but remember that anger is a step in the grief process and not its endpoint. This process will benefit you, but you're not done just because you've written everything down.

Step 2: Identify Your Emotions

In order to continue the process, you have to actually identify your emotions. We recommend that you move past basic words like *anger*, *sadness*, and *disgust*, as those represent only surface-level feelings. What you experienced typically goes far beyond a superficial wound, and it therefore requires a more complex response. You aren't just angry. You probably feel betrayed. And that's a much richer ordeal than can be expressed by a simple word. In the same way, you need more intricate language than *sadness* to express what probably is actually the feeling of *victimization*. Similarly, *disgust* doesn't go far enough to describe what you felt. You were *embarrassed*.

By choosing more sophisticated words than the basic emotions, you will begin to uncover more than what you may have thought. This whole time, you may have thought you felt rage toward the church, but the companion emotion behind that rage might have been shame. You probably expressed that rage to the church, or at least talked about it with someone else, but you might not have dealt with the shame, and it's past time that you do. For us, it wasn't until we realized there were secondary emotions involved that we began to truly heal. Most of the feelings we initially express when we go through pain are self-protective more than self-actualized. The anger many of us have toward the American church is a reaction more than a response, and it's not what's really going on. It's a surface-level backlash meant to shield ourselves from the real pain going on underneath.

It's not that these emotional expressions are wrong. It's that they're not the whole story. Your anger is probably justified. But that's just one feeling that may be happening to you. You may be feeling helpless to form a new identity on your own, insignificant because you put so much stock into a Christian identity, only to have it pulled out from underneath you, or empty because you were told you were filled with a Spirit you no longer enjoy or experience. This is where journaling, group discussions, and other therapeutic exercises come in so handy. Most of us don't come to these realizations easily, and very rarely on our own. We need to talk it out so we can fully explore the issues at hand.

There's another thing that's really crucial here. It's not enough to simply say how you felt then. You have to express what you're feeling now. For many of us, a great span of time has elapsed since the emotional and spiritual injuries that compelled them to leave church first occurred. We may no longer be enraged, but we may be bitter, skeptical, or dismissive, all of which are still functions of the initial anger we felt. That emotion got old and crusty, but it's still there, lingering under the skin. Odds are that if we were to talk about what happened and how we still feel, those more immediate emotions would return. It's by bringing them back up to the surface that we can really begin to deal with them, which leads us to the third step.

Step 3: Cancel the Debt

We have to warn you: This step is the hardest one. At least, it has been for us. For us, it meant having difficult conversations with people we were utterly enraged at and because of whom we were totally humiliated. We had developed a numbing indifference toward these people and their churches, but the more we worked through our feelings, the more we realized we had to finally hash it out. To be fair, that doesn't always have to happen in person. The other person or church doesn't necessarily need to know that you're going through this process. But you do need to go through it, and likewise, you need to tell someone that you are so they can hold you accountable to this step.

You may not believe in Jesus anymore. We get that. But there are still some things to learn from him, even if you don't think he's the savior of the world. For one thing, his message of forgiveness of our enemies is especially crucial to understanding who Jesus is and what change he tried to bring to the new community he was creating. He says to "love your enemies and pray for those who persecute you" (Matthew 5:44), but for Jesus, this isn't mere lip service. He doesn't just think this is a nice idea for us all to get along and seek peace. No, he puts his body, his very death, on the line for it. While he's being crucified, Jesus looks down at the people responsible for his brutal execution and prays, not for their untimely deaths or that God smite them from heaven, but rather, "Father, forgive them, for they do not know what they are doing" (Luke 23:34). Jesus didn't just say to love your enemies; he lived it. He wrote a blank check of forgiveness and paid for it with his own body.

We can write that check too. This is where bringing out that journal can be helpful again. Over all that stuff you wrote outlining the offenses the church or someone at the church gave you, take a big, red marker and write "Paid in Full" or "Canceled" over the words. If you have a stamp that says as much, this is the time to use it. You can even burn the journal of your grief and hurt in a cleansing fire, knowing that what you wrote can no longer hurt you again. You can be set free from this pain forever, if only you will let it go.

Step 4: Set Boundaries

Now, that doesn't mean you should just hop back into an environment where you can get hurt again. You need to decide what you need to do to protect yourself. If that means never going to a church again, we understand that (though we lament it). If that means not attending that one church again, we totally get it. You need to establish boundaries that will protect you from the hurt you received so you can live on in the forgiveness you have freely given.

For some people, this simply means avoiding the kind of church they grew up in. As we expressed earlier, there are many options out there. By all means, choose a type of church that guards against what hurt you or believes different things about that issue. There are plenty of alternatives. If you're divorced, going to a church that belittles your experience or makes you feel shame for that divorce will just set you up for more pain. Choose instead to go to a church that extends grace to your situation. This doesn't necessarily excuse you from wrong actions, and you shouldn't attend a church that gives you a free pass for bad behavior. But it does mean selecting a community that sees your situation with the lens of God, namely, that you're a forgiven human being with a heart for his mission to heal the broken. Any church that wishes to partner with you in that mission is worth your time.

For other people, the boundary needs to be more person-oriented. You might need to avoid a certain type of pastor, for example, who reminds you of the one who initially offended you. This is most common with the entrepreneurial preachers of many church plants who come off with a tinge of aggression in their teaching, as this is reminiscent of some of the fierce anger expressed by the fire-and-brimstone preachers many of us left. But it's also the small group leader who seems too friendly with your kids, reminding you of the abuse a Sunday school teacher carried out on you. Whatever the case, while you don't need to carry forward your legitimate outrage at the sins of others into new church relationships, it's important to know what your triggers are.

For still others, the boundary they need to draw is more situational. Maybe you need to avoid a few kinds of musical or preaching styles. Or perhaps you need to avoid certain topics altogether and excuse yourself from circumstances where you find yourself reliving your traumas. If you were berated by an old pastor for asking tough questions, it may be wise only to ask those questions in trusted relationships rather than in open groups, for example.

And therein lies the real solution to all of this: trust. If you're going to forgive church enough to give it another try, we recommend you find the most trustworthy Christians you know and attend their church with them. That way, if there's any fallout from what happens there, you're not on your own. You'll have a solid relationship to fall back on. You can ask your questions, express your doubts, and voice your concerns in a safe space. It may be advisable, toward this end, for you to attend a good small group before going back to a Sunday morning service so that you can have more and deeper relationships as you go deeper into church.

Finally—and this is critical—don't seek the approval of people at church. It's tempting to put yourself back into the position of being a child in that setting because you grew up in a church. As a child, you always sought affirmation from significant or powerful people to make you feel welcome and important. This set you up to be hurt because that vulnerability almost categorically gets taken advantage of by opportunistic would-be leaders who just want a following. It's important that you don't do that again. Whatever you end up doing at church, make sure to find your true identity in becoming more of the loved-by-Jesus, image-of-God, fully realized human you were born to be and not in someone else's opinion of your fitness for church.

Step 5: Make a Commitment to Forgive

Finally, we have to emphasize that forgiveness is not a one-time event. Just because you've decided to cancel the debt doesn't mean that all your emotions concerning it have gone by the wayside. Hardly. Instead, you have to make a commitment to continue forgiving. Just like you need constant grace from Jesus, the church may need such grace from you. Thus, in order to fully heal and move on, even if you never intend to go to church again, you've got to find a way to go through this process.

If possible, do this publicly. Find a way to share both what the church did to you to harm you and your efforts to forgive it. You'd be amazed at the dividends this pays. Like we said, you're not nearly the only person to have been hurt by this institution, even within the walls of a church, and the power of forgiveness is in its ability to uplift people. So if you can find a willing church, small group, or publication to work through your pain and to express your mercy, take advantage of it. You'll be shocked how many people will come up to you and thank you. We know because it's happened to us.

The next commitment you have to make is not to use what the church has done to you as a weapon against it in the future. By forgiving, you're abandoning your right to call in the church's debt to you. When you find yourself still feeling angry, you may have to revisit this commitment. You have the right to be angry, but "in your anger do not sin" (Ephesians 4:26). We sin in our anger when it no longer serves a righteous purpose. If your anger frees yourself and others from an oppressive and legalistic regime, that's awesome. But if your anger just fuels bitterness and judgmentalism, then it has no place in a whole heart. At that moment, you're contributing to the same problem you think you're solving. All that does is perpetuate evil just so you can feel better.

It's on that point that we have to say this: Forgiveness is not a feeling. Many people just want to feel like they've moved on and therefore deny that they feel anything. But true forgiveness isn't an emotional state at all. It's a choice. You don't just get over it. You get through it. It's a journey, not a destination. You may not always feel as if you've forgiven the church, just like you may not always feel love for your spouse, but just like with the spouse, love and forgiveness are choices you make. Perhaps those choices are even more potent when they're made without feeling like it in the moment. We seriously doubt Jesus felt like forgiving his executioners when he was beaten, humiliated, flogged, and crucified, but forgive them he did, and that has made all the difference.

Further Questions

1. What people do you need to forgive from your past experiences with church? What institutions?
2. What steps, if any, have you taken on this journey of forgiveness? How have they gone?
3. When you think about church, what feelings come up for you? Be specific and name as many as possible.

14

Hunting for Unicorns

If you've gotten this far, and you've made it through the tough work of forgiving the church as an institution and the people there, you may be considering going back to a church. Maybe not. Maybe you never will. We understand. But if you do want to go back, you don't want to visit just any church. You want to visit an ekklesia where you can find some real healing and undergo some valuable growth. How do you find such a church?

We used to think this was impossible. We had been to so many churches with such high hopes, only to be let down time and again by infighting, power-hoarding, and sabotage. Finding a true ekklesia felt like finding a unicorn. No such church of legend could exist, right?

Well, then we found one. Then we found another, then another. And once you discover a unicorn, you can't go on not believing in unicorns anymore. They are out there. They're probably more common than you think. As it turns out, being a community of profound consolation and restoration really is possible among human beings. It will never be perfect, and you should abandon hope of finding a morally or spiritually immaculate church. Such a body does not exist. You wouldn't want to go to a church like that at all. It wouldn't be messy enough to help you deal with your pain and work through your sin. Your very presence would mess it up. Plus, if a church seems too good to be true, it probably is, and you've been let down too many times for us to want you to go through that again.

So what should you look for? As it turns out, we have eight suggestions.

Recommendation #1: Forget about Programming

It's tempting to go to a church because of its programming. They have a great kids' ministry, and you want your child to be well taken care of, for example. We get that. Safety and fun matter for your children, and you should at least check that the environment is clean and protected. That's essential. You may also want there to be a decent musical service, entertaining and relevant preaching, or a solid hospitality experience. Free coffee is a plus.

But we suspect that the church that burned you had all or most of those things. Nearly every church strives to produce excellence in its programming and ministry efforts. They're not usually lazy. There's a flurry of activity going on at churches all around the country on any given Sunday morning, and even throughout the week. Churches, especially church plants in the last decade, have gotten good at greeting, serving, playing music, and having excellent coffee. That's all been factored in, which is part of why all those churches feel the same. That formula works to get people to come back. First-time guest retention is what they're after, and they know how to get it.

We argue that this isn't enough. It's great to have a good first-time experience, but we are deeply cynical of saccharine churches. The smiles are too big and bright, the music is too perfect, and the sermon is too funny. The other shoe has to drop at some point. The question, then, is how you force the other shoe to drop so you can peek behind the veneer. How can you tell if the programming is for real or if it's all just cheese?

It's surprisingly simple. Ask the people who go there why they attend that church. Seriously, go up to a total stranger (like the greeters at the door) and ask. If they mention the programming, then the programming is the heart of the church. That's icing. If they talk about the relationships they've formed and the friendships they've forged, then programming is just the element that brought them all together. That's the cake. The programming is often the reason a person comes back to a church the second time, but it's not why they come back a fourth or fifth time. They likely returned because they made a connection with someone, whether that was in small groups or just someone they kept seeing on Sunday mornings.

It's important here that you don't ask why they started going to that church, but why they continue to do so. Ask what they love about it and what their experience has been like. If they talk all about the excellent music or the practicality of the sermons, that might be a clue that the church doesn't run very deep. Not always, but most of the time. It's okay for them to like a church's programming, but it's not okay for that to be the key reason they go. Excellent programming is a means to an end, not the end itself. So figure out what the end is by asking multiple people why they love their church. If you get canned answers, then, by all means, keep looking.

Recommendation #2: Check the Culture

Nearly every church out there has its beliefs and value statements on its website. We used to check these out before we went to a church, but we found ourselves being too judgmental and ignoring churches unfairly. So we recommend checking these things after your first visit, perhaps right when you get home. Seriously, we would have entirely missed a high-quality unicorn church if we had checked out its website first.

But once you've gone, start with the value statements. Most churches have these. They sound like this: "Community is where life change happens and we grow" (from an actual church). Okay, that sounds good. We like the idea of that being true. But did you hear anything about that while you were there? Did the sermon mention that? Did the announcements highlight small groups that focus on that? When you asked that greeter what they liked about the church, did they mention the community at all? What was the focus while you were there?

Every church doesn't have to hit every value statement every week. But if they aren't being mentioned and rehearsed by multiple areas of the church, then they're not really values. They're just kitschy phrases, cliché without substance. However, if their values came out in the sermon, were clear by the way you were approached, and were reinforced by how the church appeared to operate, then you may have found a good one.

Next, check the church's beliefs. We should note here that it's important not to only attend churches where you agree with the belief statements. We have never found a church we fully agree with, theologically or biblically. Never. And you likely won't, either. The trick here is to see what they mention and to infer why they mention it.

For example, nearly every church is going to have a statement about the truth of the Bible. Most of those statements include the word "infallible" or the phrase "without error." That's a tough pill to swallow for most people, ourselves included. (This topic is ripe for discussion, but we can't fully explore it here.) That phrase is problematic for many, but it shouldn't be grounds to ignore the church. What might be grounds for that is what else they include. For example, some churches throw in an addendum that sounds like this: "Because it is inspired by God, it is truth without any form of error (including scientific and historical.)"

We took that sentence from an actual church, and do you see the problem? The problem isn't that they believe the Bible to be true. The problem is that they seem unwilling to discuss the matter. The fact is that not even all Christians agree on the idea of the Bible being factual when it comes to science and history. That's definitely up for debate, but in just one parenthetical phrase, they've eliminated from their potential audience anyone who has a differing opinion on the matter. They've staked their claim about something that is well within the realm of good discussion. And that's trouble.

On the other hand, we know of another church who puts it this way: "The Bible is the inspired word of God, our source of truth that leads to the best life possible." All of the core theology is intact in that it mentions both divine inspiration and truth, but the church clearly holds room for people who have differing opinions on the scientific and historical veracity of the scriptures. It might be okay there for one person who believes in a literal six-day creation done six thousand years ago to sit next to another person who believes that the early chapters of Genesis represent symbolic metaphor and not literal, scientific fact. Those two ideas can coexist within that church, and that's what we're looking for: diversity of thought.

Again, it's important to make this determination after you first attend and not before. In most churches, stuff like this doesn't come up very often. If you're there, and the community is solid and the relationships are real, then this stuff may not even matter. Just like it's important for the church to be diverse and to submit to one another out of love, it's also important for you to be diverse and to submit to other people even your idea of what is true. That's what you want from a church, so you have to be willing to live up to that calling too.

If they have a belief that truly troubles you, then keep looking. But if there's just a matter of theological discrepancy, give it an honest shot.

Recommendation #3: Pretend You Were Never a Christian

This one's going to sound odd, but our next piece of advice is to pretend you don't know anything. You may have grown up in church and may know your Bible backward and forward. And you may already know the songs they're singing, even if it's been a while. But seriously, pretend you don't know any of that.

Instead, view everything through the lens of a first-time guest who knows nothing about Jesus or church practice. Just think as if you're a typical unchurched American. You know the name of Jesus, and you know what Christmas and Easter are generally about, but you don't know a thing about what to do if you actually go to church. If you can, try to witness the experience through those eyes. Let it be awkward and weird. Let the appalling strangeness wash over you.

Here's what to look for. Do they immediately tell you what to expect? If they recognize you as a guest (which is somewhat likely), do they tell you where to go and what to do once you get there? Is the environment clean and inviting? Pay attention to the language people use. While "the blood of the Lamb" makes sense within Christianity, doesn't it sound weird and cultish to be "washed" in it? That requires some explanation before they use the phrase. Even things we Christians often take for granted, like resurrection from the dead, the primacy of the Bible, and the word *blessed*, often spin the heads of non-Christians. Does the church go out of its way to soothe those problems?

There's a reason this matters. A church that focuses on the first-time guest experience and invests in making sure they understand what's going on is likely a Gospel-loving church. By that, we don't just mean they appreciate the message of Jesus. We mean that they care about its traction and their mission to spread it. If they're making sure things are fully accessible to first-time, non-Christian guests, that means that their congregants are actively seeking out new people to engage with the Gospel. Whether you personally like the Gospel or not, this means that the church is on a mission for Jesus. It's much more likely to be authentic in its approach and to actually mean what it says. It's substantially more likely to accept free thinkers, to hear open questions, and to listen to diverse voices like yours. A Gospel-obsessed church doesn't just love Jesus. It loves people, and that means you can find a place there.

Recommendation #4: Abandon Comfort

Speaking of finding a place there, most people seem to think that implies that they're going to fit in, whatever that means. We speak from experience when we say that this is both unlikely and more than a little overrated. If you're looking for a cozy social experience, then join the Rotary Club. We hear they're quite welcoming. But we argue that what you want from a church is an uncomfortable experience. We're not saying it should be awkward or that the whole message should be impenetrably strange. What we are saying is that the best church experiences are the ones that stretch you and reform you into a new person.

Which would you rather have—a forgettable Sunday worship service with an alliterative three-point sermon you've forgotten about by the time you get home, or a life-changing, value-shifting experience that rocks your identity? If you want the former, then there are tons of regular horses out there. But if you want a unicorn, you have to be willing to let yourself get stretched, and that means choosing discomfort over comfort. It means submitting to teaching instead of necessarily rebelling against it just because it upsets you. And it means being open to the idea that your life needs to change. If you're unwilling to let yourself get transformed, then you don't want to be part of an ekklesia any more than the church you left did.

So you've got to abandon comfort and let yourself be open to renewal. That means being vulnerable, if only to yourself, to the notion that you are, in fact, a broken mess in need of help. Even if you don't think that Jesus is the answer, certainly you must agree that your brokenness is best worked out in a community of people who love you and want the best for you. Maybe you can find people, among family or friends, who will hold you accountable and have compassion for you at the same time. That's possible. But we think the church is uniquely suited to this task, even if you never decide about Jesus.

To do that, you have to give up on the cozy notion that you're going to fit in perfectly or that it's going to be a convenient experience. The best sermons are the ones that hit you to your core, and the best small groups are the ones that get you to open up and be real about your pains and misgivings. So if you want actual life change, if you want to deal with your mess, then look for an uncomfortable church. Look for one that challenges its attendees, not by bashing Bibles against their heads but by confronting people with the truth about where they stand versus where they want to stand and then graciously showing them the way back to themselves. If a sermon or small group gets you to change your vocabulary on an issue or gets you thinking about it differently, you're on to something and should consider going back.

Recommendation #5: Listen First, Judge Later

Perhaps the hardest thing for you to do will be to suspend judgment. That's hard for us too. It's all too easy to sit, snipe, and snark, folding your arms across your chest and demanding that the church impress you. Newsflash: You won't be impressed if you come in with that attitude. You'll invariably hear things that will perk your ears up in a bad way. Some of what they say may remind you all too much of what you heard as a teenager and what drove you to leave in the first place. Some of what they do will trigger you. That's almost bound to happen. Not because they're the same awful place that hurt you, but because sometimes things sound the same but mean different things. That ex-boyfriend who cheated on you told you he loved you all the time, so it's harder to hear that with the next boyfriend. That doesn't mean the next boyfriend's love is any less real. It just means it's harder to hear.

So when the church says "personal relationship with Jesus Christ," and that's a trigger for you (as it is for us), we recommend that you listen first and judge second. Listen first because they may mean something different behind it than the way you heard your original church use it. They may not mean a trite daily Bible reading and quiet time that you exercise every morning or else feel guilty about. They may instead mean the give-and-take between the human and the divine that we seek out in community and reach out for with everything we have. When they say they want to pray for you, they may not mean starting a gossip chain like the churches you grew up in. They may legitimately want to take your request before God on your behalf.

This is important because what that church says matters. It's not enough for you to pick the words out of their context and tear them apart. We know you're good at that (we are too), but that's not a healthy approach to any relationship. Our best comparison is to treat this like a first date. It's not fair to impose all your previous relationship baggage on that first experience with a new companion. You've got to be open to the idea that this person is different from the ones who hurt you, burned you, and left you. You've got to relax, have fun, ask good questions, and save your judgments for later. You shouldn't get caught up in the theater of it all, but you should listen hard and be open to new possibilities.

Treat church experiences the same way. Don't expect your first attendance to be the end-all-be-all or to deal with all of your church baggage at once. It both won't and can't. Instead, realize that the church will only help you along that journey, not be the redeemer of your past. It's a system, not a savior. So you've got to come with both ears and heart open. If it's possible, turn off your cynicism for just a couple hours and see where an impartial mind can carry you. Don't just write a church off for one or two sentences that flash on your radar. Give it an honest shake, and see what happens.

Recommendation #6: Be Realistic about Expectations

This one we can't stress enough. Churches are never going to be the fulfillment of your spiritual journey. They are companions on the path, not the destination. You can't honestly expect a church to meet all of your spiritual needs, much less to deal with all of your emotional baggage. It can't do that any more than a first date can automatically get you over a bad breakup. You know that feeling when you're in a good relationship but you're still carrying the mess from a previous relationship, and it still hurts from time to time? That's what church is going to be like. It can't solve the problem for you.

Do you remember in a previous chapter when we talked about the responsibility pie chart? You may have only been responsible for 5 percent of the problem there, and correspondingly, you have to own that 5 percent when you try a new church. Just showing up might be a huge concession for you. But you've got to own your growth and step up to the challenge of dealing with your junk. Maybe it's that you need to come back a second week so you can give the church an honest shot now that you've worked out your need to be cynical on the first try. Maybe it's that you need to try a small group instead of complaining about not making any new friends there. And maybe it's that you need to have a cup of coffee with someone you met there so you can build on that relationship instead of going it alone.

Whatever it is, own your 5 percent by being realistic about your experience at church. You can't expect the church to be perfect any more than they can expect you to be. You shouldn't stop going there just because the singer is a little off-key, the soundboard technician lets some feedback slide, or the pastor is a little unclear on a particular point. No church is perfect, so stop expecting one to be. If your willingness to try again is limited by a pristine expectation, you'll never really let yourself commit. Don't let perfect be the enemy of great. Unicorns can be muddy and blemished and still be unicorns. Judgmentalism is probably something you hated about the churches you used to know, so don't become like them by becoming snooty yourself.

Recommendation #7: Make the First Move

On that note, just like with a possible new romantic relationship, don't get left behind just because you wouldn't reach out first. Many single people seeking romance are so afraid to say, "I love you," first for fear of rejection that many great relationships fall apart before they can ever materialize, all because neither partner would take the first risk. Churches have a hard time reaching out in this way, too, and you should look for churches that are good at it. It's not at all easy for people to walk up to total strangers, start a conversation, and make a real connection in less than five minutes. And that's frankly all they get. Good churches are highly intentional about this and cultivate a culture that invests in approaching fresh faces. If you can find a church where people seem to naturally come up to you, greet you, and ask about you, particularly if it's more than one or two people, you may have found a unicorn.

But at the same time, perhaps the burden falls on you to make the first move. Even unicorns can be skittish sometimes, but that's nothing they and you can't overcome together. Sure, a good church will have people who naturally reach out to you, but you have to see if from their point of view too. If they are a good church, then they're constantly having an influx of new people, which means it may be difficult for them to realize who's new and who's not. And little is more awkward than introducing yourself to someone you've already met. To avoid that trouble, even seasoned greeters may not recognize you as a fresh face and may, therefore, avoid talking to you for that reason.

So take the burden off them and introduce yourself to them. Think of it as a party. It's loud, crowded, and uncomfortable. But if you're not willing to speak up and make yourself known, you're going to spend the entire time standing in the corner eating chips and dip and not meeting anyone. People aren't coming up to you, not because they don't want to, but because you're holding onto a negative posture. So break the tension by walking up to people and introducing yourself. It will be much more informative as to what the church is really all about, and you'll probably have more fun, anyway.

Recommendation #8: Bring a Friend

Our final recommendation is to have a friend come with you. This is a person you can bring with you who has a different set of eyes than yours. They'll catch things you missed, and they'll have a different approach to meeting new people. This can be a spouse or family member, but we recommend bringing someone else along too. This way, you'll have a whole different perspective about what went down on that particular Sunday morning.

On the one hand, this can be a bit tricky. It's somewhat too easy to slip into groupthink and just become two people taking potshots at the church together, letting your cynicism feed each other's snark. That can be dangerous and unproductive. But on the other hand, if you both try to go in with an open mind, you'll each see something a little different. Commit to acting both together and separately, and take good notes that each of you can come back to later. These notes should be good things, bad things, and ugly things, or just general notes about the environment, people, events, or the sermon. Ask each other good questions about the experience, like *What was your favorite part?* Or *What did you learn today about that church?* And just see where your conversation will take you. Sometimes, you'll just look at each other and raise eyebrows, knowing that isn't the place for either of you. And sometimes, you'll smile at each other and see the good about the place you're in. Either way, it's a ton more fun than going alone. The shared experience will bond you more than you think it might.

And that's the whole point about church. It's a shared experience. It's something we all come into together. The church is supposed to be a holy space, but that doesn't mean it's self-righteous or self-important. It means that it's set apart as a special community of people just trying to figure out life together by following Jesus in the best way they can. It's not about perfection; it's about progress.

You may notice that some of our advice doesn't deal with churches themselves, but with your attitudes and issues. There are some nuggets in there about what to avoid and look for, but much of what we have to say is about managing your attitudes and expectations. That's because if you sit there leaning back with arms crossed and a snarl on your face, it won't matter if you've found a unicorn. You'll just think it's a silly and mundane horse with a horn duct-taped to its forehead. But if you go in with a willing heart that believes there's even the slightest hope of finding a real unicorn, well, we know they exist. And we hope you'll discover one too.

Further Questions

1. Which of these recommendations is the most helpful to you? Least helpful? Why?
2. If you were to go to a church, what would you be looking for specifically? Write those things down and consider them honestly. It's hard to know if you've found something good if you haven't defined what good looks like to you.
3. What expectations do you need to leave at the door? What attitudes do you need to shed before going into a church? What about your past do you need to deal with before going back inside a Christian community? In short, what's your 5 percent?

15

The Last Remnant

Early on in the book, we talked about the great calamity that's befallen the American church and how after great disasters like that, God always leaves behind a faithful remnant. It might be easy to assume that we mean those people who are still left in the church. That's true to an extent. There is definitely a wonderful population of Christians who still go to church and seek its well-being. But who we're talking about here are the people who left the church due to its waywardness but haven't yet abandoned their principles. They may not go to church. They may not tithe or read their Bibles. And when asked, they may not even call themselves Christians. But they are true to their word, honest, wholehearted, real, and even God-fearing. They long to live good lives, and when presented with an honest choice, we think they would choose the Christian community, if only that community would prove itself worthy enough to have them.

Many who are left in the church feel abandoned by their culture. They've watched the spiritual world char into ashes around them. Endless violence, community tension, pride, greed, lust, vile dishonesty, and oppression—they continue to be rampant, all while the church they love loses its impact and prominence. It would be so easy for these people to wall themselves off in despair and try their best just to live and die in peace. They even have a biblical example of someone doing just that: Elijah.

Elijah was absolutely beside himself with grief. His nation, Northern Israel, had fallen deep into spiritual chaos. Brutality and despotism were everywhere. The king and queen were idolatry-infected tyrants who were cruel and unjust at every turn. Elijah had publicly admonished them and even executed the priests of their false gods, leading to his being chased out of the country. With a death sentence on his head, Elijah fled into the wilderness and had it out with God. He yelled, he screamed, he shouted, and he raged. He got all his grief out.

This story is recounted in 1 Kings 19 and is reflected upon in Romans 11. You see, with everything we've said about the American church, it would be easy to think that God had rejected it just like he did ancient Israel. They were torn apart by foreign warlords, moral acquiescence, and spiritual capitulation. Perhaps that's what we're seeing now with the American church. They had their day, but now it's over, and God wants to wipe it clean and start anew. It'd be easy to think that.

But Paul, the author of the letter to the Romans, thinks otherwise. "God did not reject his people" (Romans 11:2), he tells us. And that's exactly what everyone would have thought, that God was simply done with Israel. It's what everyone was waiting for. It's even what Elijah probably wanted on some level. He might have deeply internalized it, but somewhere down in his heart, Elijah wanted God to simply be finished with ancient Israel. God, after all, had every right. The nation as a whole, and its leaders in particular, had so ruptured the relationship between God and humans that

God would have been well within his character to do away with the whole notion of his kingdom.

That's exactly what Elijah preaches to God when he's asked. He says, "The Israelites have rejected your covenant, torn down your altars, and put your prophets to death with the sword. I am the only one left, and now they are trying to kill me too" (1 Kings 19:10). In other words, he's the last person standing. He's the last vestige of righteousness, but faith in the one true God has all but been snuffed out. This is Elijah left with nothing but his knees. He gets asked by God—twice—what he is doing there, and he gives that same answer each time. He's utterly despondent, beyond even a hope of hope.

But God sends him right back the way he came. He tells Elijah to go about his duties as a prophet, anointing kings and other prophets to do God's work, even at the expense of his own life. But it's in this story that we're given a glimpse into something astounding. Something amazing. Something earth-shattering. Every time we come across this sentence, we stop in our tracks. God looks out from his holy mountain at Israel in the distance and oversees all its hundreds of thousands of souls (many estimates have it around 1.5 million at this time), as numerous as the stars in the sky. Elijah thinks that the whole nation has gone down the latrine and is against him. But God says, "I reserve seven thousand in Israel—all whose knees have not bowed down to [idols]" (v. 18). Seven thousand. That sounds like a lot, but it's less than 0.5 percent of the whole nation. It's an infinitesimal portion.

But it's God's portion.

Our whole nation may be on its way to destruction, but there's a fraction, just a tiny smidgeon, that will get left behind as hope. We don't know how large that portion is. It could be 10 percent. It could be 50 percent. It could be just 0.5 percent. But we believe with all our souls that there is a portion left that is God's chosen remnant in our nation today. Notice God's requirement here. These people weren't the most religious, law-abiding, temple-attending, holiday-observing, rule-following sorts. There were possibly loads of

Israelites in those days who kept the religious traditions and kosher laws. That's not the remnant. The remnant, according to God, was the people who, despite having all sorts of social, personal, and even political pressure to do so, still did not worship the idols of their day. They didn't have enough of a voice to be heard, and they didn't have the safety to be open about their resistance, but in the privacy of their own home, when the lights were off, they worshipped God alone.

This is exactly the remnant we see now. They may not be church attenders. They may not believe what we expect. They may not vote, act, spend, believe, or live the right way, but in their heart of hearts, they have reserved their souls for God. The world around them, and even many Christians, said that power was the true god, but they didn't believe in power. The world around them, and even many Christians, said that money was the true god, but they didn't believe in money. The world around them, and even many Christians, said that sex was the true god, but they didn't believe in sex. Their hope, however small, was placed in the God of heaven, even if they could barely bring themselves to whisper his name. The remnant is so small and so out-shouted that they may not even hear enough to know God in any form that the religious elites would recognize, but still, their souls abide.

Paul calls this the "remnant chosen by grace" (Romans 11:5). Now, Paul rarely has a careless word, and you won't find one in that phrase, to be sure. The first word is *remnant*, which we have explored in this text, but we must make another note of it before passing it by. The Greek root word behind it is *leipō*, which is often translated as "lacking" or "forsaken." As we said, that's not a careless word, for this is exactly how most people in this category feel: left behind.

But what seems like abandonment is merely a prelude for the miracle. The same people who get left behind, who seemingly get totally forsaken, are also chosen. This book is not interested in the debates surrounding predestination, but what does interest us is that God chooses people. Not for salvation or damnation necessarily (that's its own rabbit trail), but for his purposes and his ways of bringing about good in this world. God doesn't choose the most religious, most righteous, or most pious people for his purposes. With even a brief scan of the Bible, you'll find that out. God repeatedly chooses the weak, the meek, the poor, the destitute, the unlearned, and even the scandalous. God chooses the least likely people imaginable to bring about the most good imaginable. We could regale you with story after story after story about God's choices, and it still wouldn't be enough.

But Paul puts it into just two words: *by grace.* You weren't chosen because of your ability to stand up and sit down at the right time during a worship service. You weren't chosen by your ability to remain sexually pure (whatever that means). You weren't chosen by your ability to follow all the rules, do all the things, and attend all the functions. You weren't chosen by your ability at all. You were chosen by grace. And that's a whole new thing to most people. It's oddly bittersweet. On the one hand, it's great because it means you don't have to do anything to join the party. On the other hand, it's awful because it means you can't do anything to join the party. You can't be good enough or holy enough or religious enough. You can't fill in a certain box on a census card and thus join in. You're not sent an invitation because you've earned one, but only because of your pre-existing relationship with the inviter. By that, we don't just mean a "personal relationship with Jesus Christ." No, we mean that a Father invited his children because he loves them and wants to spend time with them. They didn't earn the right to be children any more than you earned your way into the earthly family you have. It's the loving act of a Father, not the spiteful act of faith.

The American church (let's put this bluntly) has really messed up, paralleling the path of ancient Israel. We brought people in like they were cattle, branded them as if they belonged to us, and rejected many simply because we thought they had blemishes that only made them fit for social slaughter. We tried to weed out anybody who didn't already conform. We saw human beings and tried to render them unto our image instead of rejoicing that they were already in the image of God. Just like ancient Israel, we became so self-obsessed that our whole system imploded. Suddenly, we're seeing ourselves in the mirror for what we are—idolaters. And it doesn't look pretty.

We stumbled, hard, tearing up our knees and hands, and gouging our faces. But thanks be to God that Paul doesn't let us stop there. He continues, "Again I ask: Did they stumble so as to fall beyond recovery? Not at all! Rather, because of their transgression, salvation has come to the Gentiles" (v. 11). Here we require a small history lesson, one you're probably aware of, but bear with us for a moment. There was enormous racial strife in early Christianity between Jews and non-Jews (Gentiles). For many Jewish Christians, the inclusion of Gentiles was a disgrace to their new social movement, and the first century of Christianity sought to work through that ethnic strife. This struggle is what transformed Christianity from being a Jewish sub-cult into a multiracial, pan-cultural phenomenon. Christianity as we know it would simply not exist if it weren't for the efforts of people like Paul. So when Paul says that Israel sinned, he's not making a new statement, but he is taking a stand on the side of the Gentile. His belief that Israel burned its opportunity to the ground is a political statement, but he takes it even beyond that. He argues that it's because Israel sinned that Gentiles even have the opportunity at grace.

Make no mistake: This is an intense social moment for Paul. Once an ethnically and ritually pure Jewish elite Pharisee, Paul now says that Gentiles are included in the blessing of Abraham, not because they have done anything worthy, but actually because Israel did something awful. Because Israel failed so spectacularly, the coming of Jesus became necessary to save Israel, but because Israel's original mission was to save the world, Jesus fulfilled that mission too, on their behalf. The original goal was for the whole world to be included in Israel's grace (see Genesis 12:2–3, Exodus 19:6, and Isaiah 42:6), but it was because they failed to reach that goal that the even better grace of Jesus came to rescue both them and all nations.

"But if their transgression means riches for the world," Paul continues, "and their loss means riches for the Gentiles, how much greater riches will their full inclusion bring!" (v. 12). Therein lies the hope. Whereas the remnant is saved by God for his purpose, this is the purpose: to save the very people who did the rejecting and sinning in the first place. That's our belief of what will happen with the American church. We will be saved, not by ourselves but by the grace of Jesus through a remnant that doesn't belong to us anymore. We will be rescued by the very people we rejected. Racially segregated churches will be integrated. Churches torn apart by musical and liturgical differences will be reunited. Denominations that ripped churches limb from limb will see those limbs grafted back onto the body. Whole communities once rejected by churchgoers as sinful and disdainful will show us how to be communities of profound consolation. The whole world will watch as the American church is molded back together in the shape of one cohesive mosaic instead of shards of glass on the floor.

As Paul puts it, "For if their rejection brought reconciliation to the world, what will their acceptance be but life from the dead?" (v. 15). This is what Christians call "resurrection power," and we usually sing about that in regards to the work of Jesus at the empty tomb. But it's that same power that raised a dead body back to life that can resurrect the American church from our spiritual hospice. We are gasping our last breaths now, but we believe that God will reinvigorate us with a new life and a new Spirit, not because we have earned it and not by our power but by the grace of God through the influx of the very people we rejected, for they have learned grace and mercy and can thus lead us in the way of God.

It won't be everyone. It won't even be most people. It might just be a tiny remnant. Maybe just 0.5 percent. That's still over 1.6 million people in the United States. And 1.6 million people united under the banner of God by the resurrection power of Jesus is enough to change the world. After all, the whole Christian movement started with just five hundred unlikely followers before it went viral. The whole world may have gone off into idolatry, the American church included, but God has reserved for himself a remnant to save even these wayward people. It is through them, the very people we have rejected and subjected unto separation from God, that we will ourselves be saved.

How does that work? How will people who aren't among us save us? Look at what Elijah was called to do by God in 1 Kings 19. From the very mountain where Elijah was spoken to by God, he goes and finds a person God appointed. The man's name was Elisha, and he was a nobody. He was plowing with oxen in the field, just doing his job. He was unassuming. Nobody would know that he secretly only worshipped the true God. He hadn't conformed to the ways of the world around him, but he didn't yet have the strength to do anything about it. Without a word, Elijah "went up to him and threw his cloak around him" (v. 19). Elisha wasn't cold or anything. He didn't need warmth of body. He needed warmth of soul. The passing of a cloak may not mean much to you or us, but it meant everything in those days. It meant that Elijah was shifting ownership of his mission to Elisha. Remember, Elijah was famous. Everyone already knew who he was and what he was about. He had a price on his head. There were probably posters around the town of his name and likeness that displayed the bounty for his life.

But Elisha, unbeknownst to anyone, was waiting for just such a moment. He had no idea if it would ever come, but he desperately wanted to chase after God with his whole heart. "Elisha then left his oxen and *ran* after Elijah. 'Let me kiss my father and mother goodbye,' he said, "and then I will come with you" (v. 20, emphasis ours). He ran. This is precisely what we think the remnant would do if they were presented with an opportunity to chase after God. They would run. Not away. Toward. They would leave their whole lives behind and pursue God's mission with everything they have.

Elijah notices immediately what this means. "'Go back,' Elijah replied. 'What have I done to you?'" (v. 20). Elijah still believes that the mission is hopeless. He knows that it will be fraught with perils on all sides and that Elisha's life will never be the same. You can almost hear the lament in his voice. But Elisha has none of it. "So Elisha left him and went back. He took his yoke of oxen and slaughtered them. He burned the plowing equipment to cook the meat and gave it to the people, and they ate. Then he set out to follow Elijah and became his servant" (v. 21).

There's no going back now. He's destroyed his entire livelihood to love God and follow his mission to speak the truth and save the world. He has nothing to return to at this point. Oxen? Dead. Equipment? Burned. He doesn't even keep some of the meat for his travels. He is the first of the remnant God left behind in Israel, the initial glimmer of hope that Elijah needed to see.

So we ask, Who will be that one today? Who of the remnant will answer the call, sacrifice their livelihood, and chase after God with everything they have? We suspect it will not be just one but a whole host of communities uniting with each other for the common cause of justice and righteousness. All they need is an invitation from those of us left in the church who still love God. All they need is for us to put our cloak around them and call them one of us. For too long, we have rejected and expunged others from our presence. Now is the time for us to reach out—no, for us to go to them—to find the first person God calls us to, and ask them to come alongside us as we pursue God.

These people will not be perfect in our eyes. They will be nobodies. They may be surrounded by communities of what we see as sin, but they are ready for something that only God can do. Given just the honest chance at pursuing God, they will run with us, burning down their livelihoods and kissing their own parents goodbye. And just like Elisha to Elijah, they will double our miracle (see 2 Kings 2:9). They won't just match us. They will multiply upon what we do.

So who's it going to be? It may be a community the American church has rejected for decades. It may be a group we have disdained or ignored. It may be 1.6 million people who haven't yet given in to the pressure to conform to the patterns of this world. It may just start with one. It may start with you.

And who will call them to this mission? Might it be the very group that has done the rejecting? Might it be the same church that has done the pushing out instead of the pulling in? Might it be the few Christians who are willing to step out in boldness, take off their cloak, and put it on someone else, someone who is desperately unworthy but is chosen by grace? Might it be you?

Further Questions

1. What does it mean to you to be "chosen by grace"?
2. In your thinking, who is the remnant that God has left in the world to save his people?
3. If you are a regular churchgoer, whom has God called you to place your cloak upon?
4. If you're not a regular churchgoer, are you ready to take up the mantle? What would it take for you to join the mission and begin saving the world, even the same people who would reject you?

Afterword

Give Peace a Chance

There's no way that what we have said in this book can begin to heal the massive wounds that we've described. We have been hemorrhaging souls for decades. That is our fault. We need to go to our knees and mourn that loss with the great grief it deserves.

But there's an opportunity. It's slim, the frailest of hopes. A fool's hope. Our hope. That hope begins with the one thing we all want in our lives, in our communities, and in our families: peace.

Peace is what we're all longing for. It's what we want our nation to have with other nations. It's what we want our politicians to have with each other. It's what we want in our communities. It's what we want in our personal lives. And it's what we want in our hearts. Peace is something that permeates nearly all people's souls. It's not just about personal safety. It's about emotional harmony and the ability to be vulnerable without fear of harm.

But peace does not come by accident. In English, our word for *peace* comes from a root meaning "pact" (Latin *pax*). It's an agreement that requires both sides to agree on the terms. From a Christian standpoint, this means that the world has to recognize that the American church has a right to speak the truth to power.

As wrong as we have sometimes been, and as often as we have been on the bad side of history, we do still have truths to speak that are meaningful and relevant to the world at large. We have tried to hold people to a higher standard, sometimes out of a pursuit of power, yes, but sometimes because of a prophetic calling that leads us to understand that the higher standard is the right standard. Where would America be without the righteous and Bible-inspired indignation of Dr. King, for example? Yes, many Christians opposed his work and the cause of racial justice, but it was biblical truth about the holiness of all people that won the day. We Christians can still preach those truths now, not only about racial injustice, but also about the unfair treatment of women who have abortions, the pain of people who go through a divorce, and the rightful dignity of the LGBTQ movement. We can speak grace and truth into those stories, embracing people for who they are while calling them to the highest possible ethical standards, just like we have done well with the communities surrounding addiction and divorce.

On the flip side of this, churches need to admit for the sake of peace that we have been wrong on so many of these issues. We're not here to debate whether or not those things are bad or sinful. We're simply saying that people matter more. The church needs to make progress on these issues instead of expecting only perfection by our own standards. We can debate until we're blue in the face about sinfulness, but if we do not repent of our sin of pushing people away, it's all for naught. There is plenty of room within our churches' walls for everyone. If a man who murdered and persecuted Christians can be the most prolific church planter and apostolic letter writer of all time (Paul), then certainly we can accept people who live by their consciences, even if we disagree with the choices made by those consciences.

To do this, both sides must "bless those who persecute you; bless and do not curse." (Romans 12:14). For those outside the church, this means not lumping all Christians in with the churches who hurt you. Yes, the system was rigged against you, and it's all too easy to condemn the whole institution. But you must seek out the good people who just want to love you as Jesus does. Sometimes, they won't know how to speak the truth into your life because they don't know how to do so with grace. Show them how with all the grace you yourself can muster. Instead of drawing a boundary that separates you just because they said the wrong thing, recognize that they're trying and give them the benefit of the doubt. As it turns out, most people aren't mean, even if they consort with people who are.

For those inside the church, this means not seeing everything as an assault on our values. We have hurt people, and they rightly want to be protected from us. We have to become communities of profound consolation, which means that everyone must be welcome. If we can look a convict out on parole in the face and welcome him into our church because he committed himself to Jesus while in prison (we've seen this happen several times), then certainly we can welcome and even empower people from groups that merely disagree with us.

Many Christians halt us here and say, "But they're still living in sin." Stop. So are you. You may view their very presence as an offense, but if you can't bring yourself to welcome them with open arms in the love of Jesus by the grace of the cross, then we maintain that the resurrection power has had no hold over you. You're the one who needs to change, not them. It's your sinfulness that stands in the way of their salvation, not their own. Jesus forgave sins even as he was being executed on a Roman cross. Surely we can do the same from the safety of our churches.

Paul goes on a few verses later, "Live in harmony with one another. Do not be proud, but be willing to associate with people of low position. Do not be conceited" (v. 16). This is the next step of peace. It's intentionally bowing before people out of reverence for the image of God that they are. It's shaking their hands, hugging them, kissing their cheek, and blessing them. It's being willing to have friends who disagree with you. Probably the best example of this that we know was the unlikely friendship of two Supreme Court justices, Antonin Scalia and Ruth Bader Ginsburg. These two had nothing in common. They weren't of the same religion, race, or political orientation. They had radically different views on every case, and by all accounts, they should have hated one another as the rest of us do. But they didn't. Instead, they could be seen going to the opera together, laughing and crying at the same time, wishing each other well, riding the same elephant, and even mourning. They found out the hard way how to "live in harmony with one another" (v. 16). They didn't consider each other lowly or out of reach. They weren't conceited when it came to friendship. They respected each other deeply, and their harmony didn't mean the absence of conflict.

Surely, we can do the same. Surely, we can find our way to reconciliation. One way to do this is, as Paul says, "do not repay evil for evil" (v. 17). Yes, the American church has harmed people, but those outside of it must not repay that evil to them. They must forgive when the church repents. If anything, it would be fitting to forgive before the church repents, to wait at the doorstep for sight of the wayward church and run toward it as it comes near. And yes, there are communities in the world that have sought to harm the American church. The church must do the same, though. We must be ready, willing, and able to forgive instead of repaying evil for evil. It doesn't matter anymore who drew the first blood. It matters who is willing to put their sword down. The community that does this first is the most like Jesus.

But Paul leaves room for the problem not to be solved. This isn't a put-your-flowers-in-their-gun-barrels moment, necessarily. We may still be too far apart for that. That's why Paul says a key phrase: "If it is possible" (v. 18).

That means that this type of reconciliation isn't always possible. It certainly isn't likely. We may try and try again and still find no common ground. The peace we seek may never, ever happen. The distance may simply be too far. But make no mistake: The distance is only far because we have made it far. That's why Paul adds another phrase: "as far as it depends on you" (v. 18). In other words, you're not off the hook. That distance needs to be covered, and the one who walks it first is the better one. Forget standing your ground. Instead, walk the distance. Too often, we hear the phrase, "defending the faith" regarding apologetics and conversations with nonbelievers. Defending it from what? Invasion by the Visigoths? And why? Because it's a foxhole that needs protecting or else we lose the war?

We posit that the faith does not need defending, but rather sharing. Too many times, we see fellow Christians trying to end conversations rather than continue them. We seem to think that people can be logicked into belief. But that understanding of faith is rooted in the idea that belief is a cognitive assent when it is, rather, an emotional and spiritual journey. Our conception of faith is not rooted in psychology or theology, but biology. The parts of the brain that deal with all decision making are the same parts that deal with emotion, and they have no capacity for language. Why are people rejecting Christianity? It's not because they don't understand it. It's because they don't feel that it's right. We can complain all we want that facts should come before feelings, but the truth is that facts only make sense in the context of feelings. Again, that's not a theological position. Rather, it's hardwired into our brains. We are primarily emotional creatures, not rational ones, and the tenets of faith only make sense when the beliefs surrounding it feel worthwhile, comforting, and peaceful.

That's why Paul continues in his statement. "If it is possible, as far as it depends on you, *live at peace with everyone*" (v. 18, emphasis ours). That concept of peace isn't based on a unified set of beliefs or a rational assent to the same precepts. It's an emotional word. It comes from deep inside the brain, where there is no construct for language. People aren't leaving the faith for cognitive reasons, though they'll often come up with them after the fact. They're leaving the faith for emotional reasons like the lack of safety, the presence of oppression, or the systemization of harm. We've met dozens and dozens of people who have left the Christian faith, and every one of their stories of departure begins with an emotional moment, not a rational one. Their brains only catch up once their hearts have decided.[2]

So we need to stop defending the faith. Faith doesn't need defense. It needs the peace Paul describes. That's why he says, "Do not take revenge, my dear friends, but leave room for God's wrath" (v. 19). That word for "revenge" (Greek root *ekdikeō*) is elsewhere translated as "legal protection" (see Luke 18:3, 5), or possibly, "do justice." In other words, making everything right in other people's minds is not the business of the Christian. Instead, we are to let God worry about all that. To our knowledge, not a single soul has ever been saved by an argument. It's not likely someone will just say, "Wow, I never thought of it that way, so I guess I'll give my soul to Jesus." Rather, this happens by the intentional building of relationships that produce in people a sense that Jesus is both powerful enough to defeat sin and yet safe enough not to smite the sinner in the process. Changing people's minds isn't our goal. Rather, we are to take special care of their hearts so their minds will follow. Thus, no one needs to change before Jesus can save them. If that were the case, no one could be saved, and the work of Jesus would have been for nothing. Instead, the work of Jesus in his death and resurrection compels a change that comes through the power of the Holy Spirit. If we could change on our own, the coming of Jesus means nothing. Therefore, we must stop trying to get people to change, instead compelling them to take a step toward the peace and love of Jesus.

---

[2] Don't think any less of these people because they made a decision using their heart before their head. So did all of us. Faith is not now, nor has it ever been, a purely rational exercise. It doesn't even start there. It always starts with trusting without seeing, and that requires the heart far more than the head. Your mind will eventually catch up to you, and we by no means suggest that people leave it at the door. We do postulate, however, as any neuroscientist and psychologist would, that emotions and decisions happen before rational cognition, and that the latter is dependent on the former for context.

That is why Paul continues by quoting Proverbs: "If your enemy is hungry, feed him; if he is thirsty, give him something to drink. In doing this, you will heap burning coals on his head" (v. 20). Our world is hungry and thirsty for Jesus. It is so obvious by its current state of turmoil and idolatry that what the world needs is the saving grace of God. Every person would have a better life and be better at life, in terms of wholeheartedness, if they followed Jesus. Thus, we Christians must feed them the love of God and provide them with the water of life. In this way, we are not "overcome by evil, but [we] overcome evil with good" (v. 21).

That pairing of words ("evil" and "good") traces back to Genesis, with the Tree of the Knowledge of Good and Evil, the eating of which ushered sin into the world. Whether we believe that story to be literally true or not, the impact of this phrasing is not coincidental for Paul. He's saying that sin is utterly undone by the peace produced by love. Our souls have been at war with sin (and with themselves and each other as a result) since the beginning of time, and Paul says this is the way out. Paul argues that loving your neighbor, feeding them, and providing them with water are the essentials to undoing sin. This is the work Jesus did by dying on the cross (see John 6:53–56), it's the work the Holy Spirit has done in our souls, and it's the work we continue to do to bring about the salvation of others.

We don't win the war by slaughtering our enemies with confounding arguments. We win the war by loving our neighbors one by one in meaningful relationships that seek their well-being, even if they ultimately reject the Jesus who loves them through us. Let us, then, seek the good of our world, even when its evils drive us batty, and let the world seek our good as well, even when we drive it batty. Reconciliation is possible, even necessary, for the mission of Jesus to continue. And we suspect that Jesus would think that the world is worth our love. After all, it was worth his.

CPSIA information can be obtained
at www.ICGtesting.com
Printed in the USA
LVHW101400220422
716970LV00015B/72

9 781664 261365